GRENADA

GRENADA:

The Untold Story

Gregory Sandford &
Richard Vigilante

MADISON BOOKS
Lanham · New York · London

Copyright © 1984 by

Madison Books

4720 Boston Way
Lanham, MD 20706

3 Henrietta Street
London WC2E 8LU England

Distributed to the trade by the Scribner Book Companies.

Library of Congress Cataloging in Publication Data

Sandford, Gregory W., 1947-
  Grenada, the untold story.

  Includes bibliographical references.
  1. Grenada—Politics and government—1974-
2. Communism—Grenada. I. Vigilante, Richard A.
II. Title.
F2056.8.S26   1984   972.98'45   84-20941
ISBN 0-8191-4310-3 (alk. paper)

*In Memory of Luckey Bernard,
Deputy Commissioner, Grenada Police Service:
A Grenadian patriot.*

Contents

*8 pages of maps and illustrations
will be found following page 84.*

Preface

The Grenada revolution destroyed itself. This fact is beyond dispute. The summary execution of Prime Minister Maurice Bishop and his closest supporters on October 19, 1983—as well as the indiscriminate massacre of scores of Grenadian citizens who had gathered to hear him—was accomplished not by the CIA, nor by the bands of foreign mercenaries and domestic "counters" against whom the New JEWEL Movement (NJM) had been warning the nation for four and a half years, but by Bishop's closest comrades in the NJM leadership itself. By this fratricidal act and by the subsequent 24-hour, shoot-on-sight curfew they felt compelled to impose throughout Grenada, the leaders of the NJM revealed the extent to which they had alienated themselves from their own people and from the ideals upon which their movement had been founded.

The reasons for this self-destruction are more controversial. Clearly there was a conflict of personalities between the two main figures in the NJM—the charismatic Bishop and the less popular but more efficient and forceful Deputy Prime Minister, Bernard Coard. Less clear is the question as to whether a deeper ideological rift underlay the personality conflict. Some observers believe that Bishop and his faction within the party were essentially social democrats who had been out-maneuvered and slated for elimination by a cabal of dedicated Marxists led by Coard.

Others, including the remaining NJM leaders, maintain that there were never any differences on basic ideology within the party. They attribute the fatal clash to the overweening ambition of Coard and his followers, or (in the case of Coard supporters) to the abandonment of "principle" by Bishop and his friends. Also, there is a question of how objective problems and failures in the programs of the People's Revolutionary Government (PRG) might have fueled tensions within the revolutionary leadership over varying policies and priorities, even in the absence of an ideological rift.

While all of these questions will be considered at length below, the focus of this book will not be on why the NJM failed to maintain itself intact and in power. The real significance of the NJM's self-destruction is not as a demonstration that its regime was not viable, since it seems clear that the party's hold on power was very strong, and it could have maintained itself in power indefinitely had it not been for some serious miscalculations on the part of its leading personalities. On the contrary, what is significant is the wealth of information the NJM and its People's Revolutionary Government have left behind, showing how a regime of this kind establishes itself in a Third World country, how it uses its power to implement its own ideological program, and how it continues to perpetuate itself in power and maintain the appearance of popular support when its policies fail and genuine support disappears.

For the documents the NJM has left behind, and the observations of individuals who survived its short rule, demonstrate that the Grenada revolution was indeed a colossal failure by the standards it set for itself. The NJM set out to liberate the people of Grenada, but it ended up oppressing them. It began its rule vowing to end foreign political, economic, and cultural domination; it ended with an effort to impose on Grenadians an alien ideology and unwanted international allegiances. It came in with a program of national unification and regeneration, and left behind a legacy of hatred, confusion, debt, and disillusionment. The NJM's failure, moreover, has implications that go well beyond Grenada or even the Caribbean. For all the unique circumstances and human foibles that helped shape the Grenada situation, the fact remains that the New JEWEL Movement was led by dedicated, intelligent, and (for the most part) well-intentioned revolutionaries who sought and obtained the aid of kindred regimes around the world in applying the lessons of "scientific socialism." In the light of what the Grenada experience reveals, the burden of proof will be on these kindred regimes to demonstrate that they have not themselves failed just as dismally to achieve the nobler goals of their ideology, however successful they may have been in applying its strategies for seizing and holding power.

We owe a deep debt of gratitude to the U.S. Department of State, particularly the Foreign Service Institute, Center for the Study of Foreign Affairs, for making our research possible and to the Secretary of State's Special Advisor for Public Diplomacy, Gilbert A. Robinson, and his staff; to the Hispanic section of the Library of Congress for its friendly and efficient help in finding published materials and to the Library of the Defense Intelligence Agency for its help in exploiting the invaluable collection of Grenada documents, which were in its temporary custody during the months following the Grenada intervention. We are equally indebted to the many people in Grenada of all backgrounds and political persuasions who, with characteristic hospitality, gave generously of their time and effort to help enlighten us about the recent events in their country. Doubtless some will differ with our interpretation of those events, but we hope all will benefit from this contribution to the dialogue. It is above all to them, the Grenadian people, that we would wish this book to be useful.

The conclusions expressed in this study are entirely those of the authors, and do not represent in any respect the official views of the Department of State or any other agency of the United States government.

ONE
Prologue

It was imperative that the President understand that this had never happened in the West Indies before. This was not Latin America or Central America. The West Indian islands were consensual democracies where the rule of law was voluntarily respected by citizens and political leaders alike—and a good thing, too, because most of the islands could barely afford a national police force, let alone an army. But that consensus was a fragile thing. Bishop had been bad enough: the first government in the history of the English-speaking Caribbean to take power by coup, cozying up to the Cubans and the Soviets, suppressing democratic institutions. Now let Bishop's murderers rule Grenada by terror—as they showed every sign of intending to do—and that fragile consensus, that democratic tradition might begin to shatter throughout the islands. A great deal could be lost, not only in Grenada but throughout the eastern Caribbean. And time was running out.

It would have been impossible to guess just by watching him —the Prime Minister of Barbados, Tom Adams, wasn't an excitable man, and as the situation got worse he seemed to grow ever more calm and deliberate—but on the afternoon of October 23, four days after the murder of Maurice Bishop, Tom Adams was growing anxious. This was the third formal meeting in as many days between him and his colleagues—the leaders of the tiny island nations of the eastern Caribbean—and the representatives of the United States. And still the U.S. was unwilling to commit itself.

Adams had been ready to move on the 19th even before hearing news of the murders. The Barbados cabinet had given him the authority to arrange a collaborative rescue mission to save Bishop. But even as the cabinet was meeting, Bishop had been on the way to his death. The Grenadian people, ever faithful to Bishop personally, despite their disenchantment with his revolution, had risen en masse to liberate Bishop from the house arrest imposed on him by his former revolutionary colleagues. They marched him in triumph to Fort Rupert, named for his murdered father, shouting "We Get Leader Back," "No Bishop, No Revo" and "Down With Coard and Communism." The garrison there, in true Grenadian style, refused to fire on Bishop or the crowd and, with no other options, handed the Fort over to their one-time leader. By Grenadian standards, that should have settled things—after all, practically the entire island had risen on Bishop's behalf.

But the revolution wasn't being run by Grenadian standards any more. Now it was controlled by people who took all that rhetoric about "ruthlessness" and a "scientific approach to Marxism-Leninism" with deadly seriousness. And with deadly seriousness a squad of loyal soldiers of the revolution, dispatched by the new leaders, raced to the fort in three armored personnel carriers. After scattering the crowd with automatic-weapons fire, they arrested Maurice Bishop and a half dozen of his closest allies, placed them up against a convenient wall and shot them dead. Except for Bishop's mistress and former Minister of Education, Jacqueline Creft. Creft they beat to death.

On the 20th, John Compton, Prime Minister of St. Lucia, had called Adams. Compton had already made up his mind. The Caribbean nations could not let the situation stand. It was too dangerous for all of them. The new Grenada would try to push the entire Caribbean community into the communist camp. He believed the Caribbean nations had to take the initiative to intervene in Grenada to restore law and order and rebuild democracy. Adams, heartened by Compton's quick reaction, immediately agreed. Within a few hours the Barbados government had authorized him to commit Barbados to intervention.

Eugenia Charles, Prime Minister of Dominica, had not needed any convincing, either. As soon as she heard news of the murders and of the chaos that was breaking out on Grenada, she knew that intervention would be necessary. As she would explain to the Americans later, the West Indian nations were all kith and kin. It would be impossible for the others to abandon any one of the islands to the sort of barbarity that had overtaken Grenada.

That night, Adams agreed to an interview with Ted Koppel of ABC News. In a move deliberately calculated to signal the seriousness of the situation to the U.S. government and to help smooth the way for U.S. action, Adams told Koppel that most West Indians were hoping the U.S. would intervene militarily. By the next day, Friday the 21st, the leaders of all the Organization of Eastern Caribbean States (OECS) nations, except Grenada—Dominica, St. Lucia, Montserrat, St. Kitts-Nevis, Antigua and Barbuda, St. Vincent and the Grenadines—had gathered at Bridgetown, capital of Barbados, for an emergency session. The OECS is a regional economic, educational, and security organization that exercises authority, within its region, similar to that wielded by the Organization of American States and the United Nations. The U.N. charter specifically recognizes the regional peacekeeping rights and responsibilities of such organizations. For that reason and because none of the eastern Caribbean countries are signatories of the Rio Treaty, the collective security agreement for much of the rest of the Americas, the OECS was the appropriate forum in which to make a decision to restore peace and order in Grenada and to quell forces that threatened the security of the region.

The OECS nations, under Eugenia Charles's chairmanship, voted unanimously that night to establish a peacekeeping force to go into Grenada and to seek the assistance of friendly countries in mounting the force. Jamaica and Barbados immediately and formally joined the effort. And that same night, Adams, along with Eugenia Charles and Edward Seaga of Jamaica, met with the American Ambassador, Milan Bish, and special State Department envoy Tony Gillespie to inform them of the decision.

In the U.S., momentum had been gathering much more slowly. Through the 20th at least, a full scale intervention was not considered a likely option. Planning for a possible peaceful evacuation of the nearly 1,000 Americans on the island had been going forward since the 13th, the day before Bishop's arrest. And on the 17th, after Bishop's arrest, a special planning group was formed under the chairmanship of Langhorne Motley, Assistant Secretary of State for Inter-American Affairs, with the President and Vice President getting periodic updates. Even then there was little doubt that, should an evacuation become necessary, it would be carried out with the full cooperation and assistance of the Grenadian government.

According to Motley, only on the 19th, the day of Bishop's murder, was the task force charged to begin planning for a possible "non-permissive evacuation." Ambassador Milan Bish, hearing reports of the disorders of the 19th, alerted Washington: "There appears to be imminent danger to U.S. citizens resident on Grenada due to the current deteriorating situation, which includes reports of rioting, personnel casualties (possibly deaths), automatic weapons being discharged, Soviet-built armored personnel carriers in the Grenadian streets and some loss of water and electricity on the island . . . AmEmbassy Bridgetown recommends that the United States should now be prepared to conduct an emergency evacuation of U.S. citizens residing in Grenada."

That same day, the U.S. Embassy in Bridgetown tried to send two foreign service officers into Grenada to assess the situation and report on possible dangers to Americans on the island. But the diplomats' plane was refused permission to land. Moreover, the Embassy in Bridgetown had sent a message to the Grenadian government the day before inquiring about possible dangers to American citizens. The Grenadian reply, received on the 19th, was curt and uninformative. The planners in Washington were deeply disturbed. Not only was an evacuation beginning to seem necessary, it seemed possible that the Grenadian government would not fully cooperate in protecting American lives.

Even worse, by the afternoon of the 19th it was no longer clear that there was a government of Grenada. Both before and after Bishop's arrest, the struggle, it had seemed, had been between the Bishop faction and an opposing faction led by Bernard Coard. But Coard had dropped out of sight. People's Revolutionary Army (PRA) head General Hudson Austin, much less well known to the Americans watching the situation, now seemed to be in charge. Shortly after Bishop's death, Austin had gone on Radio Free Grenada to proclaim that a Revolutionary Military Council was now in charge of the country. The Council was not a government, but would form a government soon. Meanwhile the General displayed a certain draconian style by ordering a 24-hour, shoot-on-sight curfew—this in a country in which many houses had neither refrigeration nor running water.

On the 20th, a U.S. Navy carrier group, including the carrier *Independence*, which was headed for the Mediterranean, was diverted to the eastern Caribbean. But a U.S. government spokesman said later that planning at this stage was still focused exclusively on the limited mission of protecting American lives. Not until the 21st, when Gillespie reported the OECS request, did American planners shift "into a multilateral mode."

Even then they moved too slowly for Adams. Of course he couldn't know everything that was going on in Washington. As it turned out, on the 22nd the President—while refusing to commit to an intervention—did order U.S. forces to prepare for that larger mission. Adams knew only that his repeated inquiries since the 21st had brought the reply that Washington had not yet made up its mind and the warning that U.S. participation could by no means be taken for granted.

Now on the night of the 23rd, here was yet another American to be convinced—the President's Special Emissary Ambassador Frank McNeil, sent down to Barbados to join Gillespie and Bish.

The White House had called McNeil in Boston late in the night of the 22nd, telling him only that he was needed immediately and that he should bring tropical clothing. He drove all night, arriving in Washington in the early hours of the morning.

5

There he was informed that owing to the gravity of the OECS request, the President wanted another look at the situation before making a go/no-go decision. McNeil was rushed to Andrews Air Force Base outside Washington, boarded a small jet from which U.S. Air Force markings had been removed, and flew to Barbados accompanied by Major General George Crist. Crist, a Marine combat veteran, was to probe West Indian contingency planning so that there would be no delay if the U.S. decided to move.

So now once more the Caribbean leaders went through the situation, responding to a series of questions put to them by McNeil. Yes, it appeared that the Americans on Grenada might be in danger, particularly the medical students at the University of St. George's, who were so vulnerable in their dormitories. Yes, resistance to the Coard faction, or the Austin faction, was growing. And yes, Grenada faced the possibility of a bloody civil war—the sort of thing West Indians, so proud of and grateful for their democratic traditions, so unused to violence, found almost too horrible to comprehend. If there should be a civil war right now, the only powers in a position to tip the outcome were communist. Yes, the Soviets were certainly fond of Coard, and Coard wasn't dead, as the Americans had thought, but in hiding. And the Cuban forces on the island were probably stronger than the entire Grenadian army. Castro had been close to Bishop and was furious about his murder. Nevertheless, it would be difficult for the Cubans to remain aloof if a civil war did break out.

Direct Soviet-Cuban involvement would threaten all the islands. As one leader explained, if the current gang were allowed to grab Grenada with Soviet or Cuban assistance, while the democracies did nothing, every power-hungry adventurer in the islands would soon discover he's a Marxist-Leninist. No, the democratic nations could not leave Grenada to chaos. It would be dangerous for the foreign nationals and cruel to the Grenadian people, and it would put democracy at risk throughout the region.

But two things in particular still seemed to worry the Americans. First there were some legal niceties. The President was aware of the OECS resolution and of its desire for U.S. assistance. But the U.S. could not move in such a grave matter without a formal written request. McNeil would send one back to Washington if it could be prepared that night. The leaders agreed immediately and had a formal request drafted as the meeting proceeded.

Adams himself felt very strongly about the legalities. He made a point of explaining to McNeil and Gillespie in painstaking detail why it was the OECS (and not CARICOM—the Caribbean Community organization—or the OAS) that had authority in this matter and why OECS was acting in accord with its own charter. By signing the OECS treaty, Grenada itself had specifically recognized the OECS as the agency authorized to preserve stability in the region. The OECS could not act if any one of the members dissented, but Grenada, without a legal government at present, could not dissent. Indeed, the entire premise of the intervention was to restore legally recognizable governmental institutions on the island.

The other thing the Americans worried about was the reaction of the Grenadian people. The Americans most definitely did not want to assume responsibility for restoring order on the island only to find their interference resented.

The West Indians assured them there would be no "Yankee go home" signs; this was not Latin America. English-speaking West Indians, far from harboring anti-American hostilities, were pro-American. Many had relatives in America and understood and respected the United States. Besides, during the demonstrations on the 19th, pro-U.S., anti-Soviet, and anti-Cuban signs and graffiti had been very much in evidence. Even before the fact, some Grenadians were looking to the U.S. as a deliverer and hoping the Americans would come through.

The meeting went on for four hours. McNeil was largely convinced by the time it was over, but he and Gillespie (who had been convinced for days) repeatedly stressed that Washington had not yet made a decision and the leaders should not presume that the U.S. would join the force. They did promise to urge upon Washington the necessity for quick action one way or another. And, in fact, by secure telephone Gillespie and McNeil told Washington that the OECS request had been formalized and recommended the U.S. move immediately to ensure surprise and minimize casualties. McNeil flew back to Washington the next day after assuring the Caribbean leaders that, though no final

7

decision had been made, the U.S. would be ready to go when the decision came. He promised them an answer by 6:00 p.m. that evening.

If there was still any doubt in Washington it was erased by two events that occurred between the late hours of the 23rd and the early hours of the 24th. On Saturday the 22nd, American Embassy personnel had finally succeeded in getting into Grenada. They had been met by complete chaos—no apparent governmental authority, young revolutionaries in the streets shooting automatic weapons into the air, a population in terror. Finally they found some of the members of the Revolutionary Military Council who claimed to speak for whatever remained of authority on Grenada. The Americans tried to negotiate the details of a peaceful evacuation.

For a day and a half they made little progress. Finally, late Sunday night, they met with Major Leon "Bogo" Cornwall and again brought up the evacuation question. Cornwall was disturbingly evasive. The Americans would not necessarily be allowed to bring in charter airplane flights. (The RMC reversed and re-reversed itself on this point a number of times). Cornwall would not grant permission for a nearby Cunard liner to dock in St. George's. In the event that the Americans should leave he would not waive customs inspection or any of the other various details that are customarily relaxed during rapid evacuations. If it took hours or even days to process all 1,000 Americans, very well, they would have to wait.

The conversation with Cornwall was the most ominous development yet as far as the fate of the American citizens was concerned. The spectre of Teheran, which had been looming over the crisis since the 19th, was beginning to take on a more definite and frightening shape. The students were not yet hostages and perhaps they would never become hostages. But, as of this conversation with Cornwall, they had been made into pawns.

The other development, on the morning of the 24th, was that Tom Adams finally established clandestine contact with Sir Paul Scoon, the Governor General of Grenada. Though Grenada has been fully independent of Great Britain since 1974, as a commonwealth country it recognizes Queen Elizabeth as Queen of Grenada.

As in Britain, the Queen normally exercises no executive authority, but she is the head of state and symbolizes legitimate constitutional authority in a way that shifting political factions alone cannot. In Grenada, as in most Commonwealth countries, her authority is incarnated in a Governor General. Maurice Bishop's New JEWEL Movement, always concerned not to appear too revolutionary, had retained commonwealth, Queen and Governor General. In the current chaos, with no regular government able to establish its legitimacy, the Governor General was the last representative of legitimate constitutional authority on the island. Should he authorize the intervention there could be no doubt of its legality. But he had been kept under virtual house arrest, in fear of his life, for the last several days and had been unable to communicate freely with the outside world.

Now, in the early hours of the morning of the 24th, "through the kind offices of a friendly albeit non-participating government," Scoon got a message to Adams — a direct request to form a peacekeeping force, including U.S. troops, to restore order on the island.

On the 21st, the day of the first verbal OECS request for assistance, the President had been in Augusta, Georgia, where he had come for a weekend of golf. After the first OECS request, security became vital and it was decided that the President should handle things from Augusta rather than cause speculation by rushing back to Washington. But early in the morning of the 23rd he was awakened with the news that the Marine headquarters in Lebanon had been truckbombed by a terrorist group, killing dozens, perhaps hundreds of Marines. He returned to Washington immediately where, that evening, he received McNeil's report. He brushed aside suggestions that the tragedy in Lebanon should delay a decision on Grenada. Over the next few hours the reports of Major Cornwall's refusal to cooperate and of the Governor General's request came in. Early the next afternoon the President gave his preliminary approval to the operation. At 6:00 p.m. he signed the final order and the West Indian leaders were informed.

The intervention was coordinated in Washington by Admiral Wesley McDonald, Commander-in-Chief, Atlantic Command

(CINCLANT), but the commander in the Caribbean was Rear Admiral Joseph Metcalf, III. His flagship, the USS *Guam*, would rendezvous off Grenada with the carrier *Independence* and the rest of her carrier group. The operation would be launched before dawn on Tuesday, the 25th.

There were four major military objectives:

1. Rescue Sir Paul Scoon, Governor General of Grenada and the last remaining link with constitutional government, from his virtual captivity in Government House in St. George's.
2. Secure Pearls Airport in Grenville, Grenada's second largest city, on the northwestern side of the island.
3. Secure the not yet completed international airport at Point Salines on the southern tip of the island and use the airport to evacuate the American medical students from the nearby True Blue campus of St. George's University Medical School. Several hundred Cuban construction workers/soldiers were barracked on the airport site; American forces would have to be prepared for stiff opposition.
4. Secure the Grand Anse campus of the medical school, two miles northwest of True Blue and evacuate the more than 200 medical students there.

There would be other work to do, but with these four objectives fulfilled, most American civilians on the island would be safe and the peacekeeping force would be in position to neutralize any remaining opposition and restore peace and order.

As things turned out, it was harder than it sounded. The first Americans on the island were a small force of U.S. Navy Special Forces: the Seals. One contingent landed on the beaches near St. George's before dawn and secured Radio Grenada to ensure that the invading forces would be able to communicate with the Grenadian people. But another contingent of about a dozen Seals, loaded into a few Blackhawk armored helicopters (the first combat use of this new machine), headed to the Governor General's residence. They were charged to ensure the Governor General's safety and to evacuate him to the *Guam* waiting offshore. With them was Larry Rossin, a young American diplomat who, despite the danger of the mission, had agreed to go in to make formal diplomatic contact with the Governor General as soon as possible.

But the Seals ran into trouble. As soon as they were lowered onto the grounds of the Governor General's residence they were fired upon—by a small contingent of Grenadian soldiers detailed to "guard" Sir Paul (but in effect keeping him under arrest). The U.S. forces overpowered the Grenadians and secured the house, but almost immediately found themselves trapped. Three Russian-built BTR-60 armored personnel carriers rolled into view, cut off the Seals' escape route and opened fire on the house. The BTRs were manned by Cuban crews—the first "live" indication of how important a role the Cuban military had assumed on the tiny island. Overhead the Blackhawks circled with their diplomatic cargo, Mr. Rossin, and were soon drawing heavy anti-aircraft fire from nearby Forts Rupert and Frederick. The copters performed well, taking round after round in their tough armor. But they couldn't expose themselves indefinitely and they couldn't drop Rossin into a combat situation. They dropped a few more Seals into the fray and withdrew to the *Guam*. The Seals, who had planned to be on the island for a few hours at most and were without heavy armament, were trapped, and the Governor was still not safe.

A dozen or so miles to the northeast, things were going much more smoothly. Pearls Airport was the responsibility of the Marines of the 1-84 Amphibious Ready Group. Four hundred of them were landed by armed helicopter from the *Guam*. The forces defending Pearls were mostly Grenadians, including some militia forces, plus a few Cubans as well. Throughout the operation Grenadian regulars displayed solid training and professionalism. They were competent soldiers, "not farmboys with uniforms" according to one civilian observer. But though they retained their professionalism, most were realistic about the futility of resisting the Americans. Those at Pearls surrendered shortly and within two hours the airport was secure.

Thirty-six minutes after the Marines moved into Pearls it was the army's turn. Five hundred airborne Rangers tackled the toughest and most dangerous objective—Point Salines. The Rangers knew there were several hundred Cubans on the airfield, and they knew they were armed though they were billed as construction workers. What they didn't know was exactly how many there were, or whether they would fight or how well. No one was sure if they were armed construction workers or soldiers doing engineering duty.

To this day, Castro has maintained that most of the Cubans were not soldiers, though both sides agree that there were some professionals there and that the Cubans were organized by Colonel Pedro Tortolo Comas, a Cuban with a brilliant combat record who had flown into Grenada only the day before.

The Rangers, in any event, would soon have no doubt about the Cubans' abilities. The plan was for 10 Hercules transports, lifting off from Fort Benning, Georgia, to overfly the airport and for the 500 Rangers to parachute in. They flew into a firestorm of machine gun and anti-aircraft fire—the Cubans had made their decision and they were well-prepared. The first plane managed to drop its Rangers on target. But the pilots of the next two planes, running into even heavier fire, veered off. They hadn't expected such ferocity and they knew they were supposed to drop the Rangers safely in what was supposed to be a low casualty operation. But the field commander in charge of the drop ordered the transports back in, knowing the risk had to be taken.

The anti-aircraft guns seemed to have been placed so that they couldn't hit targets coming in at very low altitudes. If the Hercules transports could come in at around 500 feet they would probably be safe. But low jumps are dangerous—tough on the paratroopers as well as the pilots. No U.S. forces had jumped from 500 feet since World War II. The Rangers did it; every man jumped safely.

On the ground the Cubans yielded the airstrip itself but barraged the Rangers with automatic-weapons fire from a position just north of the runway. Several Rangers fell wounded. Despite the resistance the airport was secured by 7:15 a.m. Over 200 Cubans surrendered, but approximately 400 others eluded the Rangers, some heading north and east, placing themselves between the Rangers and the Grand Anse campus of the medical school.

By 8:50 a.m., the Rangers had reached and secured the True Blue campus just east of the runway. The medical students were safe and grateful. They helped the Rangers establish an emergency field hospital to treat American, Cuban and Grenadian wounded. The next wave of American forces were due in at around 10:00 a.m.: 750 troops of the 82nd Airborne whose transports would land directly on the airstrip. The Rangers cleared the runway of debris, tightened their hold on the airport and returned the fire of those Cubans still in range.

When the Airborne troops came in, the Cubans reasserted themselves. Several armored cars moved into range and opened fire on the deplaning troops. At least two men from the 82nd were killed. The ground commanders had to call in air support from the carrier *Independence* to drive the Cubans back. But by late morning the first two objectives, Pearls Airport and Point Salines, were solidly in American hands. The next two would be much tougher.

There were still no American forces in position to relieve the Seals trapped with the Governor General. They had been holding off the Cuban and Grenadian forces surrounding the house for more than six hours. Several were wounded already, ammunition was limited and would begin to get low very soon, as would the batteries for their radios. Back on board the *Guam*, Larry Rossin, worried about both the Governor General's personal safety and the political and diplomatic difficulties for both Grenada and the United States should Sir Paul be killed, stayed in close radio contact with him. Rossin, a middle-echelon careerist, was the only American in contact with Sir Paul—a point that would become important later when some observers accused the Americans of twisting the Governor General's arm to get his written invitation to the OECS to intervene in Grenada. In fact, according to Rossin, no American diplomat had an opportunity to speak with the Governor General until after Rossin, once Sir Paul had been rescued, greeted him and received the written invitation the Governor General had already prepared.

At the Grand Anse campus the situation was just as serious. There were at least 200 American students there and the plan had been to get them out quickly. Every hour that passed increased the possibility that they would be exposed to the havoc of battle, taken hostage by the desperate Grenadian Revolutionary

Military Council, or even slaughtered in a final fit of fanaticism.

By early afternoon, it was clear that there would be no quick rescue of the Grand Anse students. Most of the remaining Cuban forces were between the Army and Grand Anse area, and the campus itself was ringed with Cuban and Grenadian defenders. By 6:00 p.m. the Americans had advanced only to the small village of Frequente, less than half the distance to Grand Anse.

Decisions had to be made. The fight was virtually over in the northern half of the island. Admiral Metcalf ordered 250 of the 400 Marines at Pearls back to the *Guam*. By 4:00 p.m. he had ordered his flagship and the rest of the Navy Amphibious Group to steam around the northern tip of the island and head down the west coast to Grand Mal beach just a few miles northwest of the Governor General's residence. At 9:30 that night 13 amphibious vehicles landed 250 Marines and five tanks at Grand Mal beach.

They landed in a defended area. Immediately to the south was Fort Rupert. Just east of the Governor General's residence were Forts Frederick and Adolphus, and Richmond Hill Prison. These were still manned, largely by Grenadian troops, and there were more troops in the path from the beach to the Governor General's residence. It took the Marines 10 hours to reach the residence. At approximately 7:00 a.m. Wednesday morning they surrounded and ambushed the enemy armored cars, secured the residence and evacuated 32 civilians including Sir Paul. Ten of the Seals had been wounded before the Marines arrived. That same morning, the Marines captured Fort Rupert after mounting a heavy aerial assault against determined resistance. Two Cobra gunships were downed in the battle.

Meanwhile, the Army forces had been inching northward along the beach from Frequente, meeting stiff resistance from largely Cuban forces, though People's Revolutionary Army troops were involved as well. From the hills to the north and east came automatic-weapons fire, rocket propelled grenades, and light artillery rounds. The fighting went on through the night and into the next day.

The more than 200 students at Grand Anse could hear the battle raging around them. Though no enemy troops had entered the barracks, the students were terrified. But they were in contact with American authorities by short wave radio. It was becoming clear that they would have to be evacuated under fire. The students were instructed to move to a group of dormitory rooms close to the beach so they would be as close as possible to their rescuers when they arrived.

At 4:00 p.m. Wednesday afternoon, Marine and Ranger units in helicopter gunships, backed by A-6 and A-7 fighters, mounted a withering assault against the Cuban and Grenadian forces surrounding the campus. The assault drove many of the defenders off and bought time for six Marine helicopters to land on the beach and evacuate the students. Flanked by Marine and Ranger troops the students raced for the helicopters. They were off the beach and headed for Point Salines within minutes.

The Army forces at Grand Anse and the Marines pushing south from the Governor General's residence into the capital city of St. George's were now only a few miles apart and had between them the last significant enemy forces. The opposition was beginning to fade.

Just about an hour after the Grand Anse evacuation, the Marines took Fort Frederick, which at one point had been heavily defended and had been the source of heavy anti-aircraft fire. It was virtually deserted when the Marines arrived. A Marine detachment was sent to secure Richmond Hill Prison, where the regime's political prisoners were still detained. They were ordered to approach with caution so as not to endanger the prisoners and in fact did not actually secure the prison until noon the next day. Other Marine detachments fanned out through the city to quiet remaining pockets of resistance.

The next afternoon, there was one more significant engagement, at Calvigny Barracks east of the Point Salines Airstrip. The barracks turned out to be an important Cuban command post and the Cuban troops there put up a fierce fight, forcing the Americans to use heavy artillery and air support to subdue the position. With the capture of Calvigny, significant resistance ceased. There was some sniping and a few minor firefights through the end of the week but essentially the battle was over. Eighteen Americans were dead, 116 wounded. Twenty-four Cubans and 45 Grenadians had been killed; 21 of the Grenadians were civilian mental patients killed when American pilots mistakenly bombed a mental hospital in St. George's. More than 700 Cubans had been taken prisoner. According to a CBS News poll immediately following the intervention, 91 percent of the Grenadian people were glad the U.S. had intervened; 85 percent believed they had been in danger under the Revolutionary Military Council; 76 percent thought Cuba wanted to take control of the Grenadian government.

Maurice Bishop's revolution was over. And only now, as the peacekeeping forces combed the island for the story of the past four and a half years, did the outside world have a chance to learn what had been going on in Grenada—for Bishop and his colleagues had always been careful to conceal their true intentions. The first discovery was the weapons. Though American intelligence and the other West Indian nations had long asserted that Grenada had been getting Soviet bloc arms shipments that far exceeded its defensive needs, the weapons caches discovered by the peacekeeping forces were still impressive: more than 9,000 automatic and semi-automatic weapons and more than 5 million rounds of ammunition, heavy machine guns, light artillery, anti-aircraft weapons, and more. There were, at the time of the intervention, approximately 3,000 Grenadians under arms: 600 regulars, the rest militia. Modest as this force was, it dwarfed the defense forces of all the other eastern Caribbean islands combined, and was certainly the largest such force ever assembled in the West Indies. Before Bishop, Grenada's regular army numbered fewer than 70 troops.

But the captured weapons were just the tip of the iceberg. More important were the captured papers: First, firm evidence of five secret military agreements between Grenada and the Soviet Union (three separate agreements), Cuba, and North Korea. These agreements and other documents indicate that Grenada was planning to build an army of between seven and ten thousand troops (regular and reserve) by 1986. Such a force would have required as many as 10 percent of the Grenadian people to be enlisted full or part time. Indeed, it is unlikely that the government could have managed to build such a force. But it clearly intended to try and its sponsors clearly wanted it to try. The documents indicate that by

1986, in addition to modern rifles for a force of 10,000, and 11.5 million rounds of ammunition for those rifles, the Soviet bloc and Cuba intended to supply Grenada:

- almost 300 portable rocket launchers and 16,000 rockets
- 84 82mm-mortars
- 12 75mm-cannons
- 60 crew-served anti-aircraft guns
- 15,000 hand grenades
- 7,000 land mines
- 60 armored personnel carriers and patrol vehicles
- 20,000 sets of uniforms
- Tents for 5,000, and more.

But in addition to the military agreements, the peacekeeping forces discovered more than 11,000 secret government or party documents. Those documents, on which this book is largely based, reveal that Bishop's revolution, which many observers convinced themselves was merely "leftist," was in fact almost fanatically dedicated to turning Grenada into a West Indian version of the Soviet Union. If anything, the Grenadian revolution was more slavishly imitative of the Soviet Union than most other communist revolutions.

The shocking thing is that the Grenadian people never knew this. As the captured documents reveal, for at least 10 years, Bishop's political movement, the New JEWEL Movement, was dedicated to bringing Marxist-Leninist revolution to Grenada. Yet Bishop and his colleagues repeatedly denied this and undertook elaborate stratagems to hide their true intentions. Even after they gained power and started to push Grenada toward socialism, Bishop and his colleagues moved carefully. Their rhetoric always allowed Grenadians to hope that the revolutionaries weren't really communists at heart.

Bishop, a big, handsome, tremendously charismatic man, who grew up with a genuine moral sense and a real desire to help the poor and the downtrodden, had won the hearts of Grenadians by portraying himself as an idealistic reformer who would smash corruption, rebuild democracy, and stand up for the common man. And, in part, the portrayal was accurate. Bishop never learned the brutality to which his ideology in theory committed him. But others—men to whom the Grenadian people would never have entrusted themselves—did. How Maurice Bishop delivered his country, and himself, into their hands is a lesson worth learning.

TWO
Background to Revolution

Maurice Bishop's revolution wasn't Grenada's first. Bishop had a predecessor, Eric Mathew Gairy: two very different men, heading very different political movements. Yet both their revolutions ended in failure and oppression and in some ways their stories are remarkably similar. And though it was by overthrowing Gairy's government that Bishop and the New JEWEL Movement seized power, and though anti-Gairyism was the strongest weapon in the NJM arsenal, Gairy's story tells much about Grenada and the Grenadians who so eagerly embraced both him and eventually Bishop.

In 1949, when Eric Gairy, age 27, returned to his native Grenada from the oil fields of Aruba, Grenada was a Crown Colony of the British Empire. As such, Grenada was ruled by a Governor representing the Crown, though the government also included a locally elected legislative council.[1] Since the close of the first world war, the islanders had gradually been gaining more influence over Grenada's government.

Partly this was due to the emergence of native political leaders like the great T. A. Marryshow. Marryshow was a great believer in democracy and constitutionalism. It was he who had led the successful fight for an elected legislative council, and who fought steadily to increase the power of Grenadians over their own affairs. Marryshow was a light-skinned, educated, middle-class West Indian whose vision was of a Grenada in which Grenadians exercised what endless varieties of British colonials have called the rights of Englishmen.

After the second world war, progress toward democracy accelerated. Britain was resolved to grant the West Indian Colonies independence as soon as they could safely handle it. But what there was of democracy and self-rule in Grenada had always excluded the vast majority of the island's population — the poor, mostly illiterate, dark-skinned blacks, descendants of slaves who scratched out a living by working on Grenada's sugar, spice, and banana plantations and by working their own small plots of land.

Until 1951, the franchise in Grenada was limited and excluded many of these people. Moreover, constitutionalist leaders such as Marryshow, even when they favored universal suffrage, did not find their natural constituency among poor rural blacks but among urban, middle-class (or at least upwardly mobile) Grenadians with at least some European heritage and blood. Poor black farmers and farmworkers were excluded not only because of legal restrictions but also because no native political leader had yet made it his business to appeal to them. Eric Gairy changed all that.

Gairy himself was black, the first dark-skinned Grenadian political leader of any significance. He was born in poverty to a father who worked as an overseer on an estate. Like many young Grenadians of his day, when he was 19 he left the poverty-stricken island with its high unemployment for somewhat wealthier Trinidad. There he found work at an American military base. Soon after he moved again, this time to Aruba to work in the oil refineries. He learned to read and write at church-run literacy classes. He got involved in the trade union movement, quickly becoming a proficient organizer, known to and disliked by Dutch authorities.[2] He might have remained in Aruba or at least away from Grenada indefinitely. But Marryshow visited Aruba and Gairy met him. That meeting reawakened his interest in his native island and he returned in December of 1949. (There is some dispute as to whether Dutch authorities actually deported him from Aruba; in any event, they did not encourage him to stay.)[3]

What happened next is difficult to explain. Certainly nothing in Gairy's short career before 1950 holds any clue to the phenomenon. Within less than two years Gairy became, without question, the most powerful man in Grenada and the most powerful native leader the island had ever seen. For his fellow rural blacks he secured economic reforms of great magnitude at an amazingly speedy pace.

He began modestly enough. Though most Grenadians could sign their names or read a street sign, real literacy was an unusual skill, particularly among rural blacks. Gairy started his campaign for social justice and political power by writing letters to government officials on behalf of aggrieved peasants, frequently succeeding in protecting their rights.

By March of 1950, just four months after his return, he had founded his first political party, the Grenada People's Party. (This would become the Grenada United Labor Party: GULP.) But his principal effort went into union organizing. He concentrated on the rural workers, mostly black, who had previously been ignored by Grenada's infant trade unions. By June he was claiming 27,000 followers. By July he had organized them into the Grenada Manual and Mental Laborers Union. In August he demanded a full 50 percent wage increase for sugar factory workers. And in October he demanded a 45 percent increase in the 82-cents-a-day minimum wage for estate laborers.

All his demands were refused. Indeed, both the Governor and the estate owners refused to recognize Gairy. But his power was such that by February of 1951 he was able to call a successful general strike. He was arrested. But the arrest only raised his standing in the eyes of his fellow blacks and the riots that broke out as a result of his arrest forced the government to release him. By March he had unleashed a campaign of mass demonstrations and arson that brought the island to a standstill. The Governor was compelled to deal with Gairy and eventually the estate owners accepted his demands completely.[4]

That same year universal suffrage came to Grenada. In the elections, Gairy's party swept six of the seven elected seats on the legislative council, and Gairy won his own seat with a huge majority. (The seventh, from urban St. George's, went to elder statesman Marryshow.)

Gairy, if he had not personally transformed Grenadian politics, at least ushered in a transformation. From now on the estate workers and peasants, previously ignored by native politicians, would be the key to political power on the island. More important for our story, though, is to understand Gairy's meteoric rise to power. It was not accomplished through systematic or scientific political organizing—indeed, in almost 25 years at or near the pinacle of power in Grenada, Gairy would never bother with painstaking organizing or systematic party-building. He built his power not on program, ideology, or organization but on direct personal appeal and even hero-worship.

His race, background, personal manners and demagoguery eventually earned him the contempt of the middle and upper classes and even of the urban workers. His disregard for law and propriety brought him into constant conflict with the colonial authorities. But his defiance of both colonial authorities and the native elite thrilled his constituents. When he was arrested his followers were delighted that their leader was seen as such a threat. He had a reputation as a womanizer, and at the polls he was especially effective with women.

He understood this personal appeal and, far from being shy about it, deliberately played on it, constantly phrasing political issues in personal terms. When, for instance, after the successful 1951 general strike, the Governor asked Gairy to stop the violence that had broken out on the island, Gairy did so. But his appeals to his followers made it clear that the key argument against violence was that he, Gairy, wanted it stopped:

> I told his excellency the Governor that I have obtained your respect and your implicit confidence and you will obey me without fail. Now don't let me down.... Take my example and be a respectful decent citizen, as I say starting now. *Let me make this point, however, everyone knows that I am a serious young man and when*

I say 'No' I mean 'No'; and when I say 'Yes' I mean 'Yes.' . . . There will be nothing to save you because *the law will deal with you most severely, and 'Uncle Gairy' will turn you down completely.*[5]

The personal style worked for Gairy throughout his political career: his greatest political victories were all won in elections in which he was able to portray himself, for various reasons, as a martyr. Not for Gairy the dry, impartial constitutionalism of Marryshow. For Gairy, political power was a personal weapon, to be used against the oppressors on the behalf of the oppressed. And though, like all such leaders, he often identified the oppressed with his political allies and the oppressors with his political enemies, his early career gives every reason to believe he had genuine concern for Grenada's numerous poor.

His constituents' approach to politics was reciprocally personal. His core constituency of poor black rural workers gave no more indication than Gairy of being interested in party or ideology. Indeed, given Gairy's decidedly indifferent performance over the years following his initial brilliant successes, they don't seem to have been much interested in results either. He was for them and they were for him. It was a story that would be largely replayed under Maurice Bishop.

Gairy won the 1954 elections, maintaining his seven seats on the legislative council. But the council still had only limited authority and Gairy was far from being the ruler of Grenada. In 1956 local rule was advanced by the introduction of the Ministerial system. Gairy took the portfolio of Minister of Trade and Production and almost immediately acquired a reputation for corruption that would stay with him, with increasing justification, for the rest of his career. In the 1957 elections Gairy supporters won a majority of votes but only two seats on the legislative council, one of them Gairy's. Even that was lost to him when the colonial administrator disenfranchised him for an election violation—leading a steel band through an opponent's political rally!

True to form, Gairy was able to turn the 1961 elections into a referendum on the injustice of his disenfranchisement. The martyr was swept into office with a solid majority. Home-rule having incrementally advanced, he now held the title of Chief Minister—but not for long. His administration was quickly consumed by fiscal corruption. Outlined in a report by the colonial administrator, the scale of the scandal earned it the nickname "Squandermania." The administrator removed Gairy's government from office and suspended the constitution.[6]

The scandal was symbolized by a piano Gairy had purchased for his official residence with 700 pounds in government funds. Gairy's detractors professed to be shocked at such extravagance in the face of the island's poverty. But Gairy retorted that his enemies were angry merely because they saw a black man living the way white people had always lived and they did not want a leader of black people to have the prerogatives and respect accorded to white leaders. Many of his constituents must have agreed, because his popularity among rural blacks was not much diminished by the scandal.

He spent five years rebuilding his power. His union won another big wage increase for agricultural workers. (One of the very few genuine benefits he had procured for his constituents since the early 1950s.) After a deeply divisive 1967 election campaign he was returned to power. But by this time local government was more than play acting. Gairy was now Premier of an "Associated State" that was being groomed, as speedily as possible, for independence. He had complete control over internal affairs.

A veteran political observer in Grenada has recalled that Gairy "was always a charming scoundrel, but as time went on the charm diminished, while the scoundrel came more and more to the fore." Gairy's rule after 1967 showed the uglier side of the man and his politics. He had always regarded the government as a tool of personal power to be used by him or against him. In the '50s and early '60s colonial authorities had used it against him. Now he quickly set about using his power to strengthen his political position, gratify his social ambition, and line his pockets.

Through various forms of patronage and corruption, Gairy acquired a string of properties and small businesses, mostly hotels and nightclubs. He began to force himself into the upper crust of society, into the midst of the people he had so long condemned and envied. He promoted his cronies and business colleagues with jobs, contracts and tax concessions, while harassing his enemies. His land reform program seized the estates of political enemies and redistributed them in small parcels to GULP favorites. Social welfare programs like free milk for the poor were channeled in the direction of "Uncle's" loyal supporters. His union grew in size and power as businessmen bowed to the Premier's insistence that they recognize it and pay the wages it dictated.

If the 1967 election had been divisive, Gairy's unfettered power did even more to divide the country into pro- and anti-Gairy forces. As the civil service was dragged into the fight by Gairy's blatant abuses of patronage, basic social services—health, welfare, education, roads and infrastructure—declined. As resentments mounted, Gairy took an all-too-familiar course. He turned the police force into a weapon to intimidate potential opponents, promoting his own protegés rapidly through the ranks and sacking a series of police commissioners. He created a special corps of hand-picked "Police Aides" as his personal shock troops, and recruited a shadowy gang of thugs that became notorious as the Mongoose Gang. In 1968 he even introduced gun control to Grenada and then used it to disarm potential enemies.

Grenada shares with the other West Indian islands not only a common currency but a common appeals-court system. This fortunate arrangement guarantees all the states a relatively independent judiciary. Indeed, before Bishop, the ultimate court of appeal for Grenada was the Privy Council of the British Empire. Perhaps for this reason Gairy never gathered many political prisoners—on the day of his ouster he didn't have one. But his police force and the Mongoose Gang did go as far as administering fierce beatings to some of his enemies.

Tensions were on the rise. Moreover, economic progress, however slow, and the increasing sophistication of Grenadian society were changing and even eroding Gairy's own constituency. As the '60s were closing, the end of Gairy's power was still a decade away. But all the roles were different now. Gairy was no longer the brash young enemy of the oppressors, white or brown. He was the oppressor and he was about to face a group of young men as angry as he had ever been and as assured of their own righteousness.

*   *   *

It was their experiences abroad as soldiers in World War I that had taught Marryshow's generation to desire political equality for native Grenadians. Gairy learned about the political potential of trade unions not in his native Grenada but in Dutch Aruba. The new generation of angry young men had also learned their lessons abroad, though under somewhat more privileged circumstances.

The young men who led the fight against Gairy in the '70s, and who in other West Indian nations led similar struggles, were largely middle-class and most of all, foreign-educated. They came of age in the era of Vietnam, the Cuban revolution, the Algerian War and various socialist experiments in the newly independent nations of black Africa.

Their experiences abroad were central to their point of view. Many had been in school in the United States at the height of the radical black power movement in which West Indians like Stokely Carmichael played a role. Others, schooled in London, chafed under the discrimination against the black community there. The heightened racial consciousness of the time became a fundamental part of their political view. The students' attempts to come to grips with the experience of discrimination were shaped by the socialist theories that dominated the contemporary intellectual scene at the British and North American universities they attended. And, because all this was going on in the atmosphere of Vietnam and the anti-war movement, their experiences included an extra dose of anti-Americanism and anti-imperialism.

The political movements these returning students founded in the early 1970s—Yulimo in St. Vincent, the Movement for a New Dominica, the Antigua Caribbean Labour Movement, and Maurice Bishop's New JEWEL Movement—were thus, originally at least, socialist, anti-imperialist (which as often as not meant anti-American), pro-black power, and nationalist. By the mid-1970s the NJM was by far the most successful.

Maurice Bishop was born in Dutch Aruba on May 29, 1944, around the same time Eric Gairy was living there and working at the oil refinery. In fact, Maurice's father, Rupert, had come to Aruba from Grenada with his wife Alimenta for the same reason as Gairy—to work in the refinery. Within a few years, however, the family had returned to Grenada. Rupert went into business in a small way and achieved modest success, enough at least to establish the Bishops in the middle class, or as the young men of the NJM would learn to call it, the petit bourgeoisie.

Though Maurice Bishop's life was far from luxurious, and his stern self-made father made it impossible for him even to contemplate becoming spoiled, Maurice was lucky enough to have advantages denied most Grenadians. He went to good primary schools. And he won a scholarship to Presentation College, the Roman Catholic school that offered the best secondary education available on Grenada.

The principal remembers him as an intelligent and likeable boy. Though he was quiet, he was popular, leading several school groups and eventually becoming editor of the school newspaper. His parents were very devout and Maurice, as a young man at least, was a firm Catholic. His belief, his education, his upbringing and the advantages with which he had been blessed combined to give him a strong conscience and a great ability to sympathize with the plight of others. In later days, his teachers were not surprised that he took up the fight to change the conditions of life under Gairy. Among the several student organizations he helped to lead was the Assembly of Youth After Truth, a political discussion group he co-founded. A tremendously effective speaker later in life, at Presentation he excelled in debate.

At age 19 he left Grenada to read law at Gray's Inn in London. Again he was popular and he showed his concern for the plight of the downtrodden, and even more than before his willingness to relieve that plight, either through political action or personal commitment.

He joined the West Indian Students Society where his brilliance as a speaker, his imposing figure (he was by this time 6'3") and his engaging personality marked him as a leader. He eventually became president. He was a leading member of the Campaign Against Racial Discrimination and the Standing Conference of West Indian Organizations. He also co-founded a legal-aid clinic for the poor West Indian community of London. After qualifying as a lawyer, he married Angela Redhead, a Grenadian nurse.

Maurice's friends and associates within the West Indian Students Society and the other organizations in which he was involved were mostly West Indian leftists. He quickly moved in the same political direction. He read Marx, Engels, Lenin, Stalin, Mao, and C. L. R. James (an influential Trinidadian Trotskyite). He also visited East Germany and Czechoslovakia briefly.

He was also influenced by Julius Nyrere's Tanzanian brand of socialism, which emphasized, at least in theory, government by decentralized people's councils. Nyrere's ideas became particularly important to Maurice. He would eventually come to view parliamentary democracy as a farce that allowed the people no practical control over the workings of government. People's councils, he believed, would allow local communities to bring forth their own leaders to solve local problems.

It is impossible to know exactly when Maurice made the transition from youthful, promising, Catholic student with an active social conscience, to career revolutionary. As bright as he was, he was not given to systematic, or even, beyond certain limits, ideological reflection. Perhaps even he could not have identified the moment, if there ever was one, when the transition was complete. But as soon as he returned to Grenada in 1970, he thrust himself into left-wing political circles, which soon became revolutionary circles—and within four years he had become Eric Gairy's most dangerous opponent.

The political situation in the West Indies had heated up even before Bishop returned home from Europe. In October, 1968, the Jamiacan government had declared Walter Rodney, a left-wing Guyanese lecturer at the University of the West Indies' Jamaica campus, a prohibited immigrant. The incident ignited protests throughout the West Indies, particularly at other UWI campuses, and it helped to set off black power riots and a soldiers' mutiny that rocked the government of Trinidad. There were sympathetic black power demonstrations in Grenada. Gairy, alarmed, went on the radio to announce that he had won black power for Grenada in 1951 and no other black power was needed. He also announced that he was going to double the police force and recruit "some of the toughest and roughest rednecks to maintain law and order."[7] But the situation remained tense.

When Maurice returned to Grenada in March of 1970, he maintained his contacts with the tight network of radical West Indian intelligentsia, into which he had been drawn in London. He participated in Grenadian sympathy demonstrations for the black power movement in Trinidad and cooperated closely with left-wing leaders from that country.

That same year he attended an important meeting of radical West Indian intellectuals who had gathered to discuss future strategies for the region. Out of that meeting, held at Rat Island off St. Lucia, came a short-lived chain of political groups called the Forum. Filled primarily with intellectuals, the various Forum groups were largely ineffectual. But Bishop did get the Grenadian Forum group into the streets for a few protest marches. (Half a dozen marchers was considered a good turnout.)

Opportunity arose in November, 1970. A band of nurses staged a demonstration in St. George's to protest poor hospital conditions and a shortage of medical supplies. Along with other more mainstream opposition groups, Forum leaped in and organized a massive protest the following month. Trouble broke out, the police attacked the demonstrators and approximately 30, including Maurice Bishop, were arrested for inciting to riot.

The arrest itself was an opportunity. Bishop was certainly one of the most talented barristers in Grenada and many of his associates were lawyers as well. He collaborated with fellow attorneys from Grenada and neighboring islands to win acquittal for all involved. The trial took seven months and garnered considerable publicity. Bishop thereby set a pattern for the immediate future. Up until the time of Gairy's ouster, Bishop and his associates again and again used their legal skills to turn Grenada's independent court system into one of their favorite forums and one of their most powerful weapons against Gairy.

The protest and the trial identified Bishop as one of the island's most important young men. It also may have helped confirm Bishop in his own mind as a revolutionary leader. In any event, from 1971 on he was involved in a steady stream of progresively more revolutionary activities.

Black power played a role. During 1971, the Forum worked with a similar fledgling group called Cribou to rally Grenadian support for an International Solidarity Day sponsored by the "Pan-African Secretariat" in Guyana. The two groups were also active in a "National Conference on the Rights of Black People" protesting racism in Great Britain.

But Bishop was pursuing more broadly socialist goals as well. In February, 1972, he helped organize a secret conference in Martinique of "progressive individuals and organizations throughout the Caribbean." The goal of the conference was to establish a new Caribbean Society. The Society would have four basic goals:

1. People's ownership of all Caribbean resources.
2. The destruction of the old class structure based on wealth, color, and family.
3. Equal distribution of all resources.
4. Equal access to education, health care, housing, etc.

Suggested strategies included "infiltration into potentially Progressive Movements, i.e., Trade Unions, Guild of Graduates." The backers of the Society hoped that it would develop a "clearing house" to coordinate radical political activities throughout the region.[8]

Also in 1972, Bishop, along with his longtime associate and fellow lawyer, Kenrick Radix, helped to found two more Grenadian political organizations: MACE (the Movement for the Advancement of Community Effort) and, a few months later, MAP (the Movement for Assemblies of the People). MAP would eventually become one of the founding pillars of the New JEWEL Movement. MAP was partly the product of Bishop's fascination with Nyrere's experiments in Tanzania; it called for replacing parliamentary democracy with a system of village and workers' assemblies.

For all these groups the main enemy, or at least the main

focus of resentment, was Gairy. For Bishop and the Forum/MAP crowd, enmity to Gairy went beyond ideology. Not only was he a brute and a petty authoritarian (as well as an anti-communist), he was a rival. Gairy had captured the hearts of the very proletarians to which MAP/Forum/Bishop intended to appeal.

Richard Jacobs, a historian who later became a diplomatic representative of Bishop's government, wrote of the educated, young radicals:

> Their contempt for Gairy and his regime carried with it elements of anti-establishmentarianism and ideological differences, but tied up with this objectification of the conflict *was a deepseated contempt for the uneducated black man who, in their view, had won the sympathy and support of the agro-proletariat on false pretenses.*[9] (emphasis added)

False pretenses or not, Gairy *had* won their support. Whatever else he was, Gairy was indisputably a man of the people, while the membership of groups like Forum, Cribou, MACE, and MAP was confined to a tiny circle of disaffected intellectuals.

The difficulty was dramatized by the next elections, held in February, 1972. Four members of the MAP circle, including Unison Whiteman and Selwyn Strachan, both of whom would become leaders of the NJM, stood for seats on the legislative council. (They campaigned on the ticket of the moderate Grenada National Party, but under their own identity as the Committee of Concerned Citizens.) Gairy crushed them. Despite the mounting tide of resentment against him, Gairy's hard-core rural constituency and the strength that patronage and corruption had bought him were more than enough to dash the dreams of any number of young intellectuals.[10]

But while the young intellectuals were being rejected at the polls, in the heart of Gairy's rural constituency a group of mostly self-educated farmers was building a movement that would become an essential tool of Bishop's revolution. A score or so of these farmers, led by Teddy Victor and Sebastian Thomas, had, for some time before 1972, been meeting to discuss political and social issues, organize cooperative farming ventures, and support candidates for local office.[11] In the beginning at least, politics was not the group's first priority. Indeed, as long as the group existed it was never reduced to a purely political organization. The minutes of the first meeting show that, in addition to the cooperatives, Victor and Thomas and their associates were interested in starting a public library, sponsoring history discussions, cultural affairs, and sports competitions. They also wanted to revitalize cooperative Grenadian traditions such as the maroon—similar to the old American house-raising—and the su-su, a kind of community bank.[12]

But the members of the group were exasperated with Gairy, and deeply frustrated by the outcome of the 1972 elections. By March, just a month after Gairy's latest victory, the group decided to organize more formally to work for social and political change. The group met for the first time as the Joint Endeavour for Welfare, Education, and Liberation (JEWEL).

Even in its new, more political form, the JEWEL was neither exactly revolutionary nor exactly socialist. It quoted Marx on the ideal communist society but it began and ended its meetings with prayer. Most members, like most Grenadians, were devout Catholics. It was vehemently anti-Gairy and hinted that force might be necessary to remove him. But it had no clear plan to take power and certainly no clear plan to abolish the existing social and political system.[13] Most of all, the JEWEL leaders were farmers who understood the real needs of rural people. They were addressing their friends and neighbors, not the anonymous "masses" who were to be the raw material for implementing a political theory.

In any event, JEWEL was an immediate success. It aroused widespread support in St. David's Parish (as Grenada's counties are called), from which the founders had come, and was soon recruiting throughout the island. By early 1973, its newspaper had a circulation of nearly 2,000 (out of a total population of under 100,000). And in January 1973, it was thrust into the public eye by an almost comic incident that nevertheless showed the potential of the organization as well as giving some hints as to its original style and intentions.

Lord Brownlow, a wealthy landowner, aroused public indignation by closing off a path giving public access to the beach through his property. The JEWEL leadership wrote him letters and sent a delegation to remonstrate with him but Brownlow would not budge. Disgusted, the JEWEL leadership announced a mock "public trial," publicized it, and gathered a huge crowd, which convicted his lordship *in absentia*, tore down the fence and marched triumphantly to the sea.[14]

Even before the Brownlow incident, Bishop and the MAP crowd had sensed the potential of JEWEL. It had a mass following; all it needed was proper direction. Bishop and his colleagues hoped for a merger of the two organizations. Unison Whiteman, a MAP leader who was from St. David's Parish and knew Victor and Thomas well, was the key. He plunged himself into JEWEL's work and soon became its president. In early 1973, he proposed a union of the two parties. Both groups agreed and at a joint congress in St. David's on March 11, 1973, the union of MAP and JEWEL gave birth to the New JEWEL Movement. The MAP delegates to the congress declared that the "single aim" of their group was "the organization of a mass movement to seize political power" and that "the strategy and tactics we must ... adopt now for this period is the mass uprising."[15]

It is unclear whether Bishop and his colleagues deliberately sent Whiteman out to capture JEWEL; certainly Whiteman was on good terms with the JEWEL leaders anyway. But several years later, after the NJM had taken power, Teddy Victor would angrily tell Bishop that his first coup was not the one that overthrew Gairy but the one that captured the strength of JEWEL for his revolution.

Calls for popular uprisings may have seemed a little strange coming from a group of young men who had just been humiliated in a popular election. But the situation changed quickly, and the issue that changed it was independence. Gairy had long been luke-warm on the subject. In the early '70s, he changed his mind, deciding he wanted full independence for the island as soon as possible. Perhaps he came to realize that independence would remove the few remaining restraints on his power. His political opponents certainly realized it, and were alarmed by the prospect of independence without fundamental reforms.

Ignoring the opposition, Gairy announced that his victory in the recent elections had given him a mandate to arrange independence, which Britain was eager to grant, without a referendum. He proceeded to open discussions with the British.[16] His decision was greeted with a storm of protest. The moderate Grenada National Party, headed by Herbert Blaize, gathered 14,000 signatures against independence. In early April, government utility workers went on strike in an industrial dispute, but the strike was soon subsumed into the independence flap. Finally, tensions boiled over into mass demonstrations. A young NJM supporter was shot and killed by police in Grenville, Grenada's second largest city.[17]

The NJM moved quickly to tie their more radical complaints to the discontent over independence. In early May, Bishop and his colleagues called a "People's Convention on Independence" at Seamoon Stadium. To a crowd of thousands they denounced any scheme for independence arranged without the consent of the people. They also announced that the people would not be bound by any constitution they had not helped to frame. And they proposed their own program of replacing parliamentary democracy with assemblies of the people. They also made their usual pitch for establishing farming cooperatives and various government-run industries. They closed the meeting with the chant "WE ARE PREPARING TO TAKE POWER! POWER TO THE PEOPLE! LONG LIVE THE PEOPLE OF GRENADA!" The gauntlet was down.[18]

Within a week, the island was immobilized by a general strike supported by everyone from dockworkers to the Chamber of Commerce, all protesting Gairy's independence policy. The NJM didn't control the strike, and couldn't keep those who did from calling it off after a week. But the strike convinced the NJM leadership that a revolutionary situation was developing.

They began to prepare. On August 1, the party authorized Bishop to enlist Bernard Coard, a lecturer in economics at UWI and a rising NJM star, to draft a manifesto setting out in detail the NJM's own program for a revolutionary Grenada.[19] When the NJM manifesto appeared some weeks later it covered 12 pages of newsprint, formatted identically to the respected and independent *Torchlight* newspaper. It detailed 33 aspects of the program sketched out at the Seamoon rally. Those included:

- An "agricultural revolution" based on redistribution of land into large cooperatives.
- Nationalizing foreign-owned hotels and housing complexes for a government-run tourist industry.
- Nationalization of banks.
- A national low-cost cooperative housing plan, the houses to be built by maroon-style cooperative effort.
- Free secondary schools, improved health care, price controls on drugs and medicine and national health insurance.
- A "nationalist, anti-imperialist, anti-colonialist" foreign policy, hostile to "racist" policies of governments such as those of South Africa, the U.S.A., the United Kingdom and Canada.
- Government based on a system of village and workers' assemblies (the latter to end "the present exploitation of workers . . . in the name of Trade Unionism").[20]

The manifesto concluded with some words on the "NJM and the taking of power." There was little hope, the manifesto proclaimed, that Gairy could ever be removed by elections. But "when power changes hands in the near future, there will have to be a provisional government made up of all major groups, without regard to favour—GULP, GNP, JEWEL," as well as representatives of workers, farmers, businessmen, students, civil servants, etc., operating "on the basis of collective leadership." Boldly the manifesto proposed a National Congress of the People "to work out the best strategy for taking power." The program was radical, but the pledge to democracy was explicit and inspiring.

Bishop and his colleagues now began planning seriously for revolution. The main weapon was anti-Gairy agitation. On November 4, 1973, they held the promised People's Congress and drew a crowd estimated (albeit by friendly observers) at 10,000. The Congress tried and convicted Gairy's government of 27 crimes against the people and gave it two weeks to resign or face a general strike. The Congress went so far as to appoint a National Unity Council "to supervise the peaceful and orderly withdrawal of the government from office."[21]

Privately, the strategy was even bolder—a coup was afoot. Bishop's notes mentioned "civil disobedience" and "mass shutdown" apparently coordinated with an effort to "take EMG[airy] in house." Particular attention was to be paid to neutralizing the police: "Police must stay home on strike; those on streets are enemies and we can take definitive action with them." The names of the most notorious police leaders were inscribed with an ominous black "X" next to them and the notation "only after 'X' will they strike." Another parenthetical note suggested using Calvigny Isle for kidnapping.[22]

But once again Gairy proved himself more than the equal of the youthful radicals. On November 18, Bishop, Whiteman and four others arrived in Grenville to coordinate their plans with local businessmen. Gairy's police were waiting for them and looking for blood. Led by Innocent Belmar, one of the police leaders that had been marked with an "X," the police beat Bishop and his friends senseless. The police then dragged them off to a small cell in the Grenville police station where they shaved their heads with broken bottles. They were denied medical attention for hours. Three were eventually hospitalized. Bishop had to be sent to Barbados for treatment of a broken jaw and facial injuries that endangered his vision in one eye. Some friends of Bishop say he never fully recovered from the beating and for the rest of his life tired easily, both physically and mentally.

The public outcry was ferocious. Grenadians are not violent people and Gairy's brutality shocked and mobilized them. The general strike Bishop had been unsuccessfully trying to arrange materialized overnight, organized by a non-partisan "Committee of 22," including businessmen, labor leaders, schools and all the major churches. The Committee demanded that Gairy's secret police be disbanded, that improper police practices be stopped, that a committee of inquiry be appointed and that Innocent Belmar be suspended pending the inquiry.

Gairy gave in to the demands and the Committee, which did not include the NJM or any political group, called off the strike within a week. But police abuses were resumed and the Committee reimposed sanctions. The island erupted in a series of strikes and protests that lasted for weeks. Tragically, in one violent confrontation between demonstrators and police, Rupert Bishop, Maurice's father, was shot and killed by Gairy's police firing at point blank range. Though he had been outraged by Gairy's brutality, Rupert Bishop was a conservative law-abiding islander who disapproved of his son's politics and posed no threat to the regime. Independence came on February 7, 1974, but the continued strikes and disturbances made the planned celebrations a dismal farce. Maurice Bishop was held under arrest during the celebrations.[23]

Although the island had risen in anger against Gairy, the NJM's attempted revolution had failed. The non-partisan Committee of 22, not the NJM, had led the struggle against Gairy. That struggle had not been revolutionary, and in the long-run Gairy rode out the storm anyway. Bishop had become both hero and martyr as well as Gairy's most powerful enemy. Compared with their hopes, however, the NJM's gains were disappointing.[24]

That disappointment was the catalyst for a fundamental change in the NJM's strategy, a change that would have grave consequences for Grenada. From April 8 through April 10, 1974, the inner circle of the party leadership met in private for intensive, secret discussions on future strategy. They decided that the revolution of '73–'74 had failed because it was run by the wrong class — the middle-class establishment that dominated the Committee of 22. The NJM had failed to organize and lead the working class as an independent force with its own tactics. This must be done in the future. They reached a clear-cut decision: the NJM must transform itself and become a fully Marxist-Leninist "vanguard" party. This decision was shared with no one outside the inner-circle of the Bureau, the executive council of the NJM. But nine years later, in his 1982 "Line of March of the Party" speech to party members, a copy of which was captured by the American Marines in October '83, Bishop spoke about the decision and the failures that had preceded it:

> [During the March '73 to April '74 period] Mistakes were made, a deep class approach was not taken, no attempt was made to build a Leninist Party, there was an over-reliance on spontaneity and the

37

possibilities of crowd politics... this was ultra-leftism in action
... the major weakness of this period was the subjective factor, the
fact that a Leninist approach to par[t]y building and to strategy
and tactics were not adopted; and this is notwithstanding the
notable achievements of the period, including the publication of
our Manifesto.

After the defeat in January '74 the Party held its first major
evaluation in April 1974, we were then exactly one year and one
month old. We spent a few days, a whole week-end, looking at the
Party and trying to decide where we went wrong and what correc-
tive action was needed. That is when we decided in theory and
principle that we should build a Leninist Party.

The decision to become a "vanguard" party on the Marxist-
Leninist model had momentous implications both for the future
international alliances of the NJM and for its policies within
Grenada. It meant, in essence, that the party would no longer
seek merely to build on existing grievances to overthrow the
present regime. Rather, an elite cadre of professional revolutionaries would educate the masses, develop their class consciousness,
encourage resentments, sharpen their understanding of their
own class interests as opposed to those of the ruling bourgeoisie,
and lead them on a revolutionary course to be charted by the
vanguard party itself. The goal would be a dictatorship of the
working class led by the party, over the defeated bourgeoisie.[25]

Henceforth, at every critical juncture, party leaders would
see the solution to their problems in a stricter adherence to
Marxist-Leninist standards: tighter centralization, more structured
organization, more-rigid application of Soviet models of development. Hence, at every step they alienated themselves even further from the aspirations of the Grenadian people. The NJM's
worries about Grenada's "backwardness" reinforced this alienation,
by compelling the NJM to defer consistently to the examples and
advice of more experienced revolutionaries in more developed
countries, who presumably had a more "mature" Marxist outlook.

In the short-term, requirements for full membership in the
party were tightened, a new category of "Fighting Member" was
introduced (at Coard's suggestion) to foster development of the
cadre, and the NJM Bureau (the party's governing body) created

a new set of field workers to help it assert more control over the party's local affiliates. The effect of all these changes was to centralize power in the hands of the leadership.

The triumph of the new party line represented the final takeover of the NJM by Bishop and the urban intellectuals of MAP. The first result was the loss of the old rural JEWEL leaders. Anticipating the trend, Sebastian Thomas had left the NJM by December 1973. Sherwyn Lazarus, another key JEWEL leader, dropped out and eventually emigrated. Teddy Victor stayed until 1976, fighting for a restoration of JEWEL's democratic ideas, but then resigned from the party Bureau. Only Whiteman, who had arranged the merger and who had been working with Bishop for two years before JEWEL was founded, remained.

If the old JEWEL leadership was no longer important to the NJM, the old JEWEL membership still was. JEWEL's chief attraction to Bishop and his colleagues had been that, unlike their MAP, it had a mass following. That following had to be retained and expanded. Accordingly, the decision to transform the NJM into a Marxist-Leninist party was kept strictly secret from the party's constituents. Most Grenadians, especially the poorer rural peasants and workers, are Catholic, socially conservative, and virulently anti-communist. They would never have supported an overtly communist political movement. Indeed, up until the time of his death, many and probably most Grenadians did not believe Bishop, to whom they were so devoted, could be a communist. When the Coard faction had Bishop arrested, many believed this represented a communist takeover.

While the Bureau leaders were studying the atheist doctrine of Marxist dialectics, NJM meetings below the Bureau level featured prayer and party propaganda, which appealed to religious sentiments. And while party theory called for raising the class consciousness of the urban proletariat, day-to-day strategy was to exploit popular causes to appeal to the rural masses. As Unison Whiteman explained at the time, "If we are to gain a 10 percent [defection?] of Gairy's support, we must move into the area of more purely emotional techniques." They would have to downplay ideological points such as the "People's Assemblies in areas like Brizan, Beaton, and Windsor Forest . . . where the people

relate more to paternalism and authoritarianism." Other suggestions included "conferring status on those who enter the Movement"; "Singing of an NJM song"; and "Experimentation with
drumming, bright lights, etc., before meetings."[26]

There was other organizational work to be done as well. The
vanguard party was to begin the "Infiltration of tr[ade] unions,
societies, service clubs, etc.' The party also created a network
of overseas support organizations to help raise money for the
NJM and "to ensure that other countries abroad understand
what is happening and would not come to Gairy's aid."[27] According to notes kept by Bishop, in a presentation on NJM foreign
policy, Bernard Coard argued that the effort to prepare the
masses for revolution and instruct them with correct ideology,
arms and training would require "links with friendly for[eign]
governments." NJM foreign policy goals would include removing
Cuba for hemispheric isolation and breaking U.S. "hegemonic
control" of the region.[28]

The new organizational and fund raising efforts paid off
quickly. Within a year or so there were party cells and support
groups in almost every village, and the party's newspaper, *The
New Jewel*, soon claimed a circulation of 10,000. Because the
NJM was careful to conceal its ideological commitments, because
its populist approach to politics rivaled Gairy's, and because
Bishop was, like Gairy, a man of tremendous personal magnetism,
who, also like Gairy, had earned martyr status, the party won a
reputation as Gairy's only effective opposition. Gairy recognized
the threat and used his power and his police constantly to harass
what he called the "JEWEL communists." But he was only helping his enemies. The harassment reinforced the NJM leaders'
image as martyrs to Grenadian liberation. And because the NJM
was chock full of skilled attorneys, Gairy's harrassment earned
him repeated humiliations in the West Indian courts.

By the time of the December 1976, elections, the NJM had
made itself indispensable to any attempt to beat Gairy at the
polls. Temporarily at least, the party had dropped its opposition
to elections. (Bishop would later cite the NJM's willingness to
join in the elections as a mark of its Leninist maturity.) It joined
in an electoral alliance ("The People's Alliance") with the Grenada

National Party and the new United People's Party. Gairy beat them again, but this time it was close. Gairy polled 52.2 percent of the vote and took nine of the 15 council seats. Of the six seats earned by the People's Alliance, the NJM got three. Maurice Bishop was Leader of the Opposition in the Grenadian parliament.

Parliament was a perfect stage for Bishop. He used his new forum again and again to make vitriolic attacks on Gairy. NJM supporters were urged to attend parliamentary sessions as an audience to what had become political theater and *The New Jewel* reprinted his accusations in full. More and more, Bishop's eloquence, anger, and force of personality (especially appealing to women) was making him the focus of opposition to Gairy.[29]

The NJM was pushing forward organizationally as well. It did charity work, distributing food parcels and running a day care center. Bishop and colleagues established the Grenada Council for Human Rights, which monitored and denounced Gairy's brutalities. The NJM mounted mass demonstrations that, pre-dictably, provoked Gairy's police thugs to violence and further polarized the country. It renewed its efforts to infiltrate the trade unions, this time concentrating on urban workers, and winning the leadership of two of the most important unions. During this period also, the party made another organizational decision, one that in later years would have profound consequences within the party. It decided, naturally enough, to make a major effort to recruit Grenadian youth into the NJM. It chose for this mission Bernard Coard and his Organization for Revolutionary Education and Liberation (OREL).

Coard had been involved with the NJM since the early 1970s. It was Coard who drafted the NJM's manifesto in 1973, and it was Coard who was responsible for many of the organizational changes made to help build the NJM into a "vanguard" party. He was uniquely fit for all these duties. Like Bishop, he was extremely bright. But unlike Bishop, his intelligence was of a systematic and analytic sort that made him both a good organizer and a good ideologue. Of all the NJM leaders, he was by far the most schooled in Marxist-Leninist doctrine and he became the keeper of the party's ideological flame. He had leadership qualities, but they were entirely unlike Bishop's. Bishop was

GRENADA: THE UNTOLD STORY

excitable and passionate and he led by inspiring passion. Without a man like him at the head of the NJM it is unlikely the movement could have gotten off the ground. But Bishop had little patience with long ideological arguments or sustained reasoned argument of any kind. Bishop was far better at delivering a quick sermon to catch the heart than a lengthy lecture to turn the head. He was a man for the crowds, not for the conference room.

Coard was amiable, although he had none of Bishop's charismatic appeal for large groups. But one-on-one or in a small group, he was extraordinarily effective. Those who knew him say that Coard would spend hours debating, lecturing and cajoling NJM members whom he believed to be mistaken about some ideological or practical point. He had a patient and reasonable manner and rarely was provoked into an ill humor. He would fully consider all his opponents' arguments and patiently answer them one by one, being extremely persuasive and always willing to go over the same ground again and again until he would finally win agreement, or at least acquiessence. He was a guru, not a messiah. And like all gurus, he worked his magic not on the inconstant crowd but on a small group of increasingly devoted and constant followers.

He founded OREL, a radical student organization, in 1975. It appealed to the young, privileged, middle-class groups which leaned towards the radical intelligentsia: students from the prestigious Grenada Boys Secondary School and Presentation College. The age and position of the membership allowed OREL to make a much more forthright commitment to Marxism than the NJM could make publicly. Its newspaper was called *The Spark* in imitation of Lenin's party organ. In the paper, these children of relative privilege called for "the total destruction of the capitalist class" and announced that "the liberation of the workers and peasants can only come through violent revolution."[30]

OREL supported the NJM in the 1976 elections. It was assimilated into the NJM shortly thereafter and was given the duty of coordinating the party's new youth program. But its assimilation was never complete. The OREL leadership, gathered and trained by Coard, shared his academic tendencies and his more disciplined approach to Marxist ideology and Leninist principles of organization. For these young revolutionaries—Liam James, Leon Cornwall, Basil Gehagen, Ewart Lane and others who rose to importance in the NJM—Coard, not Bishop, was leader, and Coard kept them close to him as a personal power base. The OREL crowd was inexperienced in grass-roots work among the people. But they were dedicated to the cause of class struggle and revolution. They became the leading advocates within the party for Marxist-Leninist standards of discipline and strict adherence to the models of the Soviet revolution. Their constitutency was not the Grenadian people, the constituency to which Bishop appealed, but rather the party organization; in the end, the latter turned out to be the constituency that mattered.

From the mid-'70s on, Bishop and indeed the entire NJM grew increasingly dependent on Coard. As the NJM grew in size and complexity, running the party became a challenging managerial task for which Bishop, bright as he was, had neither talent nor, especially, inclination. Coard was not only brilliant and a natural organizer; he was a workhorse, perhaps even a workaholic, whose attention to detail rarely flagged. Faced with increasingly complex decisions and ever higher stakes as the revolutionary movement prospered, Bishop, who had great respect for Coard, came to regard him as indispensable.

By late 1978, the frantic organizing of the previous two years had borne fruit. The NJM was ready to take power. It was certainly the most powerful political force on the island. But its strength was not merely political. Its ties to Cuba, Guyana, and Michael Manley's left-wing government in Jamaica and radical parties throughout the Carribbean gave it important sources of financial support. It had organized a small clandestine military wing, for which Cuba and Guyana were able to supply training. (In fact, the NJM's increasingly close relations with Cuba, as well as its refusal to make a public declaration abjuring external communist alliances, caused the practical dissolution of its electoral alliance with the GNP and the United People's Party [UPP]. At home, though, party propaganda repeatedly denied that the NJM was a communist organization.) NJM infiltrators had been placed in the police, the Defense Force, and even Gairy's nightclubs, and were providing detailed intelligence on when and how Gairy might be overthrown. It is not clear exactly when the decision to oust Gairy by military coup was made, but by the end of 1978, the NJM was ready to move.[31]

NOTES

1. A. W. Singham, *The Hero and the Crowd in a Colonial Polity* (New Haven and London: Yale University Press, 1968), pp. 103–108.
2. *Ibid.*, p. 155.
3. *Ibid.*
4. *Ibid*, pp. 155–171.
5. *Ibid.*, pp. 165–166.
6. *Ibid.*, pp. 172–188.
7. W. Richard Jacobs, "The Movement Towards Grenadian Independence," in *Independence for Grenada—Myth or Reality?* (St. Augustine, Trinidad: University of the West Indies, Institute of International Relations, 1974) p. 23.
8. Guidelines for Caribbean conference in Martinique, February 11–15, 1972 (Grenada Documents, unnumbered). These documents, hereafter abbreviated GD, were taken into custody by U.S. forces at the time of the joint U.S.-OECS intervention in October 1983. At this writing they were still being held in a U.S. Department of Defense facility pending their return to the government of Grenada. Where possible, documents are identified by the preliminary catalogue numbers assigned by DOD personnel; otherwise, they will be shown as "unnumbered."
9. Jacobs, "The Movement," p. 23.
10. Richard Jacobs and Ian Jacobs, *Grenada: The Route to Revolution* (Havana: Cas de las Americas, 1980) pp. 97–98.
11. Conversations with JEWEL co-founder Teddy Victor; handwritten minutes of JEWEL and early NJM meetings supplied by Teddy Victor.
12. Conversations with Teddy Victor; minutes of JEWEL meetings, various dates. The maroon is a tradition very much like a rural American barn-raising, in which everyone contributes a little food and effort to help a neighbor complete a major building project such as a house or barn. A su-su is a sort of folk banking arrangement whereby members all make regular contributions to a common fund, and each takes a turn collecting the total amount.

13. Various issues of *JEWEL* (organ of the movement); minutes of JEWEL meetings, various dates.

14. Minutes of JEWEL meeting, January 7, 1973; conversations with Teddy Victor.

15. Minutes of JEWEL meeting, January 7, 1973; "A Review of the Organisational Structure of the NJM. Paper to be presented to the 1st International Conference of Grenadians to be held in Grenada from 23rd–26th August 1974" (MS written in Maurice Bishop's hand [GD, unnumbered]). Unless otherwise specified, all handwritten documents referred to appear to be in Maurice Bishop's hand.

16. Jacobs, "Movement Towards Grenadian Independence," pp. 26–27; Bernard Coard, "The Meaning of Political Independence in the Commonwealth Caribbean," in *Independence for Grenada*, p. 70.

17. Jacobs, "Movement Towards Grenadian Independence," pp. 27–28.

18. "Proposals to the People's Convention on Independence, Seamoon, Sunday, May 6th, 1973" (GD unnumbered).

19. Jacobs, "Movement Towards Grenadian Independence," pp. 28–29; "NJM and the People's Charter" (GD unnumbered); minutes of NJM meeting August 1, 1973.

20. "Manifesto of the New JEWEL Movement for Power to the People and for Achieving Real Independence for Grenada, Carriacou, Petit Martinique, and the Grenadian Grenadines," undated.

21. Letter from NJM publications secretary E. E. Carberry addressed to "Dear fellow Grenadians," dated November 7, 1973 (GD, 001644); D. Sinclair DaBreo, *The Prostitution of a Democracy: The Agony of Grenada* (published by the author, n.d.), pp. 22–24; minutes of NJM meeting August 22, 1973.

22. Handwritten notes on a meeting of the National Unity Council, 6 November 1973 (GD unnumbered). A police report of a search of Bishop's residence conducted on February 6, 1974 claimed to have found a plan "with instructions outlining how the Honourable Premier should be assassinated at his business place, 'Evening Palace,' at Grand Anse. . . . " (GD 103241).

23. Jacobs and Jacobs, *Route to Rev*, pp. 100–101.

24. Conversations with Lloyd Noel (former NJM legal advisor and Attorney General under the People's Revolutionary Government), Eric Pierre, and others.

25. "The Struggle for Democracy and against Imperialism in Grenada," interview with Maurice Bishop and Unison Whiteman which appeared in the Cuban weekly *Bohemia*, August 19, 1977, reprinted in Bruce Marcus and Michael Taber, ed., *Maurice Bishop Speaks:*

The Grenada Revolution 1979–1983 (New York: Pathfinder Press, 1983), p. 18; "Line of March for the Party Presented by Comrade Maurice Bishop, Chairman, Central Committee, to General Meeting of the Party on Monday September 13, 1982" (GD 001560); Chris Holness, "The Political Situation in Grenada" (GD 100467), pp. 9–10; handwritten notes on meetings of the NJM Bureau April 8–10, 1974 (GD 005377).

26. "Documents of the NJM Weekend Assess-In," 22–23 June 1974, pp. 13–14 (GD 005377).

27. Notes of Bureau meetings, April 8–10, 1974; "Main Problems Confronting the NJM in Its Work Within the Working Class Movement—A Historical Analysis" (GD 101095), pp. 2–3.

28. Handwritten notes of a meeting during the NJM Bureau Assess-In of June 22, 1974 (GD unnumbered).

29. Jacobs and Jacobs, *Route to Rev*, pp. 112–113; "Unfair and Unfree Elections—Grenada, 7th December 1976" (NJM propaganda sheet); conversations with Winston Whyte (UPP candidate in 1976 and later M.P.), Teddy Victor and others.

30. Handwritten notes on an NJM meeting, December 16, 1976 (GD unnumbered). *The Spark*, vol. 1, no. 2 (mid-late 1975?).

31. Conversations with Teddy Victor, Kennedy Budhlall, and others; Jacobs and Jacobs, *Route to Rev*, p. 117.

THREE

The New JEWEL Movement Takes Power

O n Tuesday morning, March 13, 1979, Grenadians awoke to the voice of Maurice Bishop over Radio Grenada:

> At 4:15 a.m. this morning, the People's Revolutionary Army seized control of the army barracks at True Blue. The barracks were burned to the ground. After half-an-hour struggle, the forces of Gairy's army were completely defeated, and surrendered. . . .

> I am now calling on the working people, the youths, workers, farmers, fishermen, middle-class people, and women to join our armed revolutionary forces at central positions in your communities and to give them any assistance they call for.

Gairy had left Grenada the previous day for meetings at the U.N. in New York. Bishop claimed that he had "fled the country, leaving orders for all opposition forces, including especially the people's leader [as Bishop referred to himself] to be massacred." He implied that the coup was necessary to forestall the massacre.[1]

There was no evidence of an impending "massacre," but Gairy was aware that the NJM was planning a coup and was trying to head it off. In February, two NJM supporters, James Wardally and Chester Humphrey, had been arrested in Washington on charges that they had been helping to run guns from the United States to Grenada. (The guns were shipped in barrels marked "grease" and had been delivered to the home of Unison Whiteman in September).[2]

Washington's investigation had forced the NJM's hand. Almost immediately after Wardally and Humphrey were arrested, the leadership made the decision to move on Gairy. Everything was made ready. On March 12th, with Gairy conveniently leaving the country, the leadership made the final decision: they would move in the next day. Bishop would give the final signal. In the early morning hours, Bishop called to give NJM military commanders the code word: "Apple." Under Austin's command, Stran Phillip supervised the True Blue barracks with a force of about two dozen men armed with small arms and molotov cocktails. Gairy's soldiers panicked and ran without firing a shot. There was one casualty, a Defense Force Lieutenant named Bizan who was called to the scene when the attack began and was killed by the NJM troops. Austin's men moved on to Radio Grenada and took it almost immediately. Soon thereafter, Stran Phillip led a bold attack on the police headquarters in St. George's. It also succumbed quickly.[4] Meanwhile, on the other side of the island, another force under Kennedy Budhlall seized Pearls Airport and the Grenville police station, and, after commandeering a school bus, set out to capture the rural police stations gathering supporters as they went. Other squads arrested Gairy's ministers, senior police officers, prison officials and "Mongoose Gang" leaders and took them into protective custody.[5]

By afternoon it was virtually all over. The coup was immensely successful: most Grenadians rejoiced. One reason was the speed and lack of bloodshed. The tensions of recent months had led many to fear that a more violent confrontation was in the offing. Now people were grateful not only that Gairy and his thugs were gone, but that the long-gathering storm had passed so quickly. Even Cynthia Gairy, the Prime Minister's wife, drove voluntarily to Radio Grenada and went on the air to plead with her countrymen not to resist but to support the new government.[6]

Bishop, in his first address as "the people's leader," used his considerable gifts as an orator to quiet fears and encourage national unity. He promised that "the supporters of the former Gairy government will not be injured in any way. Their homes, their families, and their jobs are completely safe, so long as they do not offer violence to our government." He also sought to assuage fears of the NJM's communistic reputation by assuring his listeners that:

> . . . all democratic freedoms, including freedom of elections, religious and political opinion, will be restored to the people. The personal safety and property of individuals will be protected. Foreign residents are quite safe, and are welcome to remain in Grenada. And we look forward to continuing friendly relations with those countries with which we now have such relations.

The revolution, Bishop concluded, was "for work, for food, for decent housing and health services, and for a bright future for our children and great-grandchildren."[7] Within a few days such unrevolutionary institutions as the conservative Grenada National Party and the Chamber of Commerce, as well as the independent *Torchlight* newspaper, had endorsed Gairy's ouster, congratulated the NJM for bringing off the coup with maximum efficiency and minimum bloodshed, and given at least conditional support to the new government.

As effective as Bishop's remarks were domestically, they were clearly intended for a foreign audience as well. The NJM leaders were aware that gaining international recognition for their government would be a difficult and delicate matter on which its survival could depend. For that reason, they had previously considered how their revolution should be portrayed to the world.

An internal policy document had discussed the importance that the government's first major policy statement would have, noting that it would be meticulously analyzed in foreign capitals, including Washington. The document noted that Washington particularly would want to be reassured that the revolution was not communist and that the new government would preserve "private property . . . individual rights [and] hemispheric solidarity."

The study had recommended that the government's first statement emphasize "moderation, care, and non-alignment" with heavy emphasis on Gairy's abuses of human rights and the constitution. The NJM should promise a return to constitutional rule "at the earliest possible opportunity," including "free and fair elections" under a new constitution.[8] As it happened, Bishop's first statement said substantially that.

It turned out to be a wise policy. Both in the regional press and among most regional governments, the very first reactions to the coup were nervous and disapproving. The NJM coup, the Caribbean papers pointed out, was the first in the modern history of the English-speaking Caribbean and it had overthrown a man who, however unpleasant, had been legally and repeatedly elected by the Grenadian people. John Compton, Prime Minister of St. Lucia, went so far as to fire off a message to London asking Her Majesty's government to intervene. Several other Caribbean governments were equally disapproving, though others, including Guyana and Jamaica, were supportive.

It was the NJM's moderation and pledges to restore democracy that turned the tide. CARICOM, the organization of the Caribbean Economic Community, voted to extend recognition to the new People's Revolutionary Government (PRG) only after George Louison, the PRG's representative, persuaded regional leaders of his government's commitment to early elections. The Caribbean press came around within a few days. The *Nation* of Barbados expressed the general feeling:

> Mr. Maurice Bishop seems clearly established as the new leader of Grenada. Already it is clear that there is an abundance of goodwill going for him, not only in the Caribbean but in the outside world . . . the future of the Bishop government is in the hands of Maurice Bishop himself. . . . His first task is to co-operate with his

many well-wishers at home and abroad in an effort to give acceptable legal status to his administration.[9]

Outside the Caribbean, the next priority for Bishop was relations with the United States. Though he and the other NJM leaders had always been apprehensive about U.S. opposition, things went quite easily at first. The U.S. Embassy in Barbados was responsible for relations with all the islands of the eastern Caribbean. Within a day of the coup, Ambassador Frank Ortiz cabled a first tentative assessment to Washington. He noted the radical ideology of the NJM leaders. But he believed that the responsibilities of power and a growing acquaintanceship with the U.S. might moderate both their ideas and their anti-Americanism. He advocated that the U.S. accept Bishop's expressed desire for a peaceful relationship. He particularly warned against the U.S. allowing itself to be pressured by other regional governments into any precipitate actions against the PRG.[10] The official U.S. view that emerged, confirmed in consultations with Britain and Canada, was that "any sanctions at this stage could be counterproductive," perhaps forcing the NJM into Cuba's arms.[11]

Accordingly, on March 22, the United States announced its intention "to continue the friendly and cooperative relations our two countries have enjoyed since Grenada's independence in 1974." The statement commended the PRG's repeated promises to hold elections and honor internationally accepted standards of human rights. On March 23, Ambassador Ortiz met with Bishop and Unison Whiteman representing the PRG. He assured them that the U.S. would respect Grenada's right to determine its own internal policies and that the PRG had made a favorable impression so far. But Ortiz also emphasized that it was the PRG's commitment to elections that had made speedy U.S. recognition possible. The elections should come quickly.

Bishop temporized. He refused to fix a date, and said that Gairy had left the electoral system in a mess. He also hinted at the NJM's continued preference for the grassroots democracy of the village assemblies. But he did say that he would make an announcement about elections in a few days and that he thought the U.S. would be satisfied with what he said. On the subject of

U.S. aid, Ortiz told Bishop and Whiteman that the U.S. was willing to continue to provide Grenada with all possible assistance, as it had in the past. Following standard procedure, most of the aid would be channeled through regional institutions such as the Caribbean Development Bank (CDB). To answer more immediate needs, Ortiz advised Bishop and Whiteman that they might be able to draw on the embassy's Special Development Assistance (SDA) fund for smaller community-based projects.[12]

Bishop and Whiteman seemed interested in U.S. aid. But as Ortiz later recalled, in this and all his other talks with Bishop on the subject of aid, the leader was non-committal and "never responded to my urgings that he initiate specific talks with us." Ortiz returned to Barbados optimistic about the possibility of a cooperative relationship, pessimistic about elections, and convinced that patience and forbearance should be the keys to American policy regarding the PRG.

On the surface, relations between the two countries were off to a good start. But within days, the inescapable imperatives of Bishop's ideology asserted themselves and the situation quickly deteriorated. On March 25, Bishop made a major speech publicly promulgating a series of "People's Laws." These suspended the constitution, "legalized" the PRG, vested the People's Revolutionary Army with full police powers and provided for preventive detention of persons deemed "likely to endanger the public safety." Two days later he told an interviewer that elections would come only after a new constitution. The most important development, as it turned out, was the PRG's repeated and intensified public warnings that Gairy, from his exile in the U.S., was planning a mercenary invasion and counter-coup. At an April 5th press conference, Bishop announced he would be seeking arms from the U.S. to defend against Gairy. On April 7 he made the request in person to U.S. embassy officials, but was vague about his requirements. Then on April 8 he told a public rally that he would request arms and aid from Cuba.[13]

On April 10, Ambassador Ortiz returned to Grenada. He was shocked to find the island in the midst of an invasion scare. In a meeting with Bernard Coard, he assured Coard that Gairy was in San Diego, not anywhere near Grenada, that his movements were being monitored, and that he presented no evident threat. Ortiz also mentioned that a false invasion scare might depress tourism. Ortiz met with Bishop in the afternoon and again Gairy dominated the meeting. He assured Bishop that the U.S. took the PRG's concerns seriously, that Gairy was under FBI surveillance, and that while Gairy was on U.S. soil he would not be permitted to undertake any activities aimed at overthrowing the PRG. Then, after reiterating that the U.S. took his concerns about Gairy seriously, Ortiz told Bishop that in the view of the U.S. government it would not be in Grenada's best interest to seek assistance from Cuba. "We would view with displeasure any tendency on the part of Grenada to develop closer ties with Cuba." Ortiz asked Bishop for specifics about the arms he had requested on the 7th. Bishop hesitated, then said he needed 500 semi-automatic weapons and 200 submachine guns. Ortiz mentioned ammunition. Bishop thought a moment, then said about 1,000 rounds for each gun would do. Ortiz then stressed once again that U.S. concerns about Cuba were critical. Finally he asked pointblank whether the Cubans had offered any assistance. Bishop replied that they had not, but Grenada would seek help from any source to ward off an invasion. Ortiz reminded him that the U.S. had only now received details of the PRG's arms request and had still not received detailed requests for economic aid. In that light, Bishop's earlier remarks about not yet having received any aid from "traditional friends" were hard to understand. They parted amicably.[14]

Bishop was lying. On April 7, eight Cuban personnel had entered Grenada surreptitiously, facilitated by the NJM. On April 9th, the Guyanese ship *Jaimito* had arrived in St. George's after dark and unloaded a consignment of Cuban arms concealed in a cargo of rice. Another ship, the *Matanzas*, departed Cuba April 6th with a shipment of arms that arrived April 14. All these weapons and personnel were either in Grenada or en route at the very moment Bishop was telling Ortiz that Cuba had not offered any military assistance.

The break came on April 13. Bishop delivered the most famous speech of his career: his "backyard" speech attacking what he alleged were U.S. efforts to dictate Grenada's foreign policy. Referring to his recent meetings with Ortiz, Bishop charged that the U.S. ambassador had:

1. uttered "veiled threats" against Grenada's tourist industry if the PRG continued to warn against mercenary invasions;
2. ignored the new government's pleas for massive aid;
3. brushed off PRG concerns about the "very real danger" of a mercenary invasion by Gairy;
4. warned Grenada against developing any relations with Cuba despite the threat of Gairy.

"We reject *entirely*," Bishop told his listeners, "the argument of the American Ambassador that we would only be entitled to call upon the Cubans to come to our assistance only after the mercenaries have landed and commenced the attack." Bishop concluded, "No country has the right to tell us what to do or how to run our country or who to be friendly with. . . . we are not in anybody's backyard, and we are definitely not for sale."[15] This speech later became the basis for the widespread view that Grenada was pushed into communist alliance by heavy-handed American bullying. In fact, the NJM's policies had been determined long before. As early as 1976 the NJM bureau had concluded that the United States was the "No. 1 enemy" that "will not let us take power without a fight. [We must] understand what we are up against."[16]

Also as early as 1976, the NJM was considering steps to involve Cuba more closely in Grenadian affairs and founded a Grenada-Cuba Association. By 1977–78 it was openly sending delegations to Cuba, and NJM soldiers were trained in Cuba and Guyana prior to the 1979 coup. There is also circumstantial evidence (but no conclusive proof) that those two countries participated in the coup itself.

Many Grenadians of all backgrounds, for instance, recall suspicious movements, occurrences in Grenada's coastal waters, and hints from people in the know, which led them to conclude that Cubans and Guyanese were present during the NJM takeover. Two people well known to Gregory Sandford, one a senior police officer, had spoken to the wife of a Guyanese sergeant in

Grenada who admitted his role in the coup. Grenada's most famous and respected journalist, Alistair Hughes, recalls being told at the time, by a source inside the NJM, that the attacking force included "forty-seven Grenadians and a few other people of whom we're not saying anything now."[17]

Bishop's speech, with its wild distortions of Ortiz's remarks, was an attempt to exploit the encounter with Ortiz as justification for a long established, but secret policy that could no longer be concealed from the Grenadian people. Bishop knew that within a very short time Grenadians were going to become aware of a massive buildup of Cuban arms and personnel.

In April, the main road from St. George's to Grenville, the island's most important artery, was closed for two weeks while the Cubans established a PRA training camp at Grand Etang Lake in Grenada's mountainous interior. The island was repeatedly blacked out and placed under curfew when Cuban ships unloaded in the harbor. For most Grenadians, these were strange and disturbing developments, and Bishop knew he would need a persuasive explanation for his actions. The threat of Gairy and the alleged arrogance of Ortiz helped prepare the ground.

This is not to say that the PRG's fears about Gairy and suspicions about the U.S. were not genuine. To some degree they were, but they were fed more by ideology and paranoia than by fact. The NJM had always expected the enmity of the U.S. Then, once the PRG had attacked the U.S. openly and had accepted arms from the Cubans, there seemed all the more reason to fear the U.S. and seek aid from the totalitarian nations.

The issue of elections gives a perfect example of the PRG's difficulties in this regard. Knowing that speedy elections were the quid pro quo for continued good relations with other Caribbean states, as well as the U.S. and the U.K., in early April 1979, the PRG went so far as to begin preparing for elections. The leaders, however, must have quickly realized that this was a point on which they could not compromise. Had they lost, they could have been tried for treason. Had they won, they would have acknowledged that their revolution was subject to challenge at the polls. This they had no intention of doing. As a Leninist "vanguard party," the NJM believed its mandate to be derived from the dialectical forces of history, not the momentary whim of an ideologically backward electorate.[18]

Their ideology thus necessarily put the NJM leaders at odds with the parliamentary democracies and led them to align themselves openly with the totalitarian powers. The election law was scrapped. Their invective against Washington heated up, no doubt partly in anticipation of U.S. reaction to their failure to hold elections. Meanwhile, Cuban, Guyanese, and eventually Soviet military aid flowed in.[19]

Short of holding elections, the NJM needed some method of bestowing legitimacy on the government so as to satisfy critics and potential opponents both at home and abroad. Party leaders did not yet feel strong enough to openly claim dictatorial power for the NJM. To cloak the character and objectives of their regime they resorted to a "strategy of alliances." Maurice Bishop later explained:

> I can remember the very first set of names we announced for the ruling council was ... made up mainly (outside of the immediate leadership), of the petty-bourgeoisie, the upper petty-bourgeoisie, and the national bourgeoisie. You remember that? Simon Charles and Sidney Ambrose—peasantry; Bernard Gittens—professional middle strata; Lloyd Noel—professional middle strata; Plam Buxo and Norris Bain—middle capitalist; Lyden Ramdhanny—big capitalist; that is who the People's Revolutionary government was. And this was done deliberately so that imperialism won't get too excited and ... wouldn't think about sending in troops.[20]

Not until a week and a half later did the NJM put in nine more party comrades, Bishop explained, and even then the NJM leaders had more sense than to admit they were Marxist-Leninists.

The bourgeois allies were not *part* of the working class dictatorship. They were tools to be used by it as the party dictated. The real decision-making positions were reserved for the NJM elite. A memo to Bureau members as early as May, 1979, proposed an immediate effort to get key members and supporters into "key positions over the next three months, to watch events and enable better control by leadership." By 1982,

Bishop would be able to tell party members: "If you look at the ruling council of the People's Revolutionary Government you will discover an over 90% direct control by the Party . . . there is absolutely no doubt that we have a hegemonic control on power and over all the capital areas of the State."[21]

As Grenadians began probing to see what rights remained to them under a revolutionary government, the NJM's insistence on a monopoly of power became clearer. Bishop's temporizing about elections was the first dark cloud on the horizon, a cloud that even according to pro-NJM accounts had begun to disquiet the people by summer. Other indications appeared. *Torchlight*, Grenada's only independent newspaper, had given its support to the NJM both before and after the coup. Yet during the spring and summer of 1979, government leaders repeatedly attacked the paper for printing articles embarrassing to the regime. On May 18, a *Torchlight* reporter's camera was seized.

The PRG's ambivalence about elections soon turned into outright repression of potential opponents. In July, the Grenada People's Party, which had maintained a critical but generally supportive stance, staged public meetings in Sauteurs and Grenville. Both times the meetings were broken up by gangs of NJM rowdies who seized the microphones and threatened the GNP speakers. Calls to the police brought no action. That was disquieting enough, but eventually word came back informally from Bernard Coard that any further meetings could lead to imprisonment for the GNP leaders. Coard later defended publicly the right of "the people" to disrupt such meetings. Without any means to protect its followers, the GNP withdrew from public political activities for the duration of the PRG regime. The NJM was now the only active political party.[22]

Tougher measures were reserved for old friends. Some of the rural leaders of the old JEWEL had never resigned themselves to the dominance of Bishop and the other urban Marxists. During the late 1970s, before the revolution, Teddy Victor had become the chief organizer and spokesman for a group of dissidents including Sebastian Thomas, Kenneth "Buck" Budhlall, Caldwell Taylor and others. The dissidents criticized the Bureau's unwillingness to submit itself to the general membership for re-election.

They demanded the party be run as the same sort of grass-roots democracy it claimed to advocate for Grenada as a whole. And it condemned the absolute control of the Marxist elite.[23]

The dissidents were not strong enough to win their reforms before the March 13 coup that overthrew Gairy. Victor went back to cooperative farming and virtually dropped out of the party, though his influence in the countryside was still strong. But his differences with the NJM were briefly subsumed in the common effort of March 13th. Victor awoke that morning to find his house surrounded by supporters of the coup looking to him for leadership. He called the temporary NJM headquarters at Radio Grenada for instructions and was told that his help was desired and expected. At the head of the crowd he then proceeded to St. David's police station and seized it for the revolution.[24]

Just three weeks later, Victor was thrown out of the party by Bishop himself. Bishop claimed that Victor and the Budhlall brothers had been planning to assassinate the NJM leadership. In fact, Victor had been meeting with the Budhlalls, Stran Phillip and others. He tried to persuade them that the party leaders were already turning their backs on the people and that the rural leaders must close ranks and press their demands now before it was too late. Despite his expulsion, Victor grew increasingly outspoken. He even wrote a letter to Bishop referring to the JEWEL–MAP merger of 1973 as "the first coup." The letter continued, "When one looks again at the maneuvers used to acquire the highly centralized power the leadership now wields in the NJM he is right to suspect that it is the same plan that is in store for the island's government."[25]

Victor's efforts to rally the rural leaders for a last stand were unsuccessful. Too many of them, including Buck's brother, Kennedy Budhlall, whose position in the army would have made him essential to any coalition, had a deep faith in Maurice Bishop. Nevertheless, by October 1979, the NJM leaders were convinced they had to move against what they regarded as a burgeoning threat to the revolution. The PRG security service (the Special Branch) believed Victor's agitation was having an effect and was part of a larger complex of counter-revolutionary activity probably backed by the U.S. Stran Phillip, who on the day of the coup had led the attacks on the army barracks and the main police station, had become unhappy with the NJM since the coup. Winston Whyte, the leading figure of the defunct United People's Party, had rebuffed attempts to secure his cooperation with the PRG and had travelled to Trinidad, Barbados, and Martinique for what appeared to be suspicious political meetings. According to another report, which the Special Branch conceded was untested, a prominent GNP official was concealing a cache of arms intended for an "armed revolution to overthrow the PRG." Security saw the police force as politically unreliable, representing "the greatest threat to the PRG." Everyone, according to the Special Branch, was upset about the Cubans.[26]

Before the JEWEL faction could be dealt with, one problem had to be solved: how to handle the inevitable reaction of the independent press to a tough, potentially violent internal crackdown. The difficulty was soon eliminated. Relations between the *Torchlight* and the PRG were already badly strained. For some time, the cabinet had been considering taking action against the paper, but there was disagreement over how aggressive the government should be. One group, including Bishop, Lyden Ramdhanny and some others, favored pressure and persuasion. Others, including Bernard Coard, favored stronger action. As time went on, Bishop himself grew less patient with the paper's independent attitude, but he took no action.[27]

As so often happened, Bernard Coard was the one who finally acted decisively. In early October, Bishop was away on a North American tour, leaving Coard as Acting Prime Minister. On October 10th, the *Torchlight* published an interview with two Rastafarian spokesmen who accused the PRG of persecuting their sect, denounced "Cuba and Russia," questioned why elections had not been held, and threatened protest and resistance against government policies. Three days later, Coard ordered the *Torchlight* closed. Bishop disapproved, but was as always concerned to maintain party unity. When he returned he publicly supported the closure. On October 20th, he announced the government's decision to "democratise the ownership structure" of the *Torchlight*. Eventually, the PRG finessed the problem by encouraging a takeover of the press by *Torchlight* employees.[28]

A pro-NJM account of the incident summed up the government's position:

> The *Torchlight's* position was that "free press" equals "free speech" and that the publishers of a given newspaper "alone had the right to determine what its editorial policy would be." The PRG's position is that the press has a national responsibility . . .

By this account the closure was not merely a reaction to specific articles or editorials, but a denial of the very idea of a free press.[29]

Outside the NJM the closure was met with outrage. Roman Catholic Bishop Sydney Charles of Grenada issued a pastoral letter warning that the denial of basic human rights would lead, as in Gairy's time, to "restlessness and rebellion." As for reaction abroad, probably no single action of the NJM was so damaging to its international image. But the closure gave the NJM what it wanted. It eliminated the principal vehicle for public dissent, and prepared the way for tighter control of Grenadian society.[30] With the *Torchlight* out of the way, PRG security could move. The very next day, the government launched a wave of arrests and detentions that continued sporadically into the following month. Among the first to be arrested were Teddy Victor and Winston Whyte, who were charged with masterminding a plot to overthrow the PRG with a campaign of terror and assassinations. Also arrested were senior police officer Wilton de Ravinere and other policemen, Dr. Rupert Japal (the GNP leader accused of hoarding arms) and Dr. Jensen Otway. Several of the Budhlall brothers were arrested, though Kennedy Budhlall, who had rejected Victor's views, was not disturbed or even removed from his position. Many of their followers, along with some leading Rastafarians, were also arrested.[31]

Security forces dutifully produced arms, ammunition, explosives, and a map which they claimed to have seized from the persons and properties of the detainees. But the way the government handled this alleged "evidence" reinforced the impression that it had been planted. On November 9th and 10th, a few young detainees were put before a camera on Grenada Free

Television and allowed to confess their role in the plot. Liam "Ouswu" James, in charge of NJM security, was behind a curtain, and his voice could clearly be heard prompting the young men through their confession. Attorney General Lloyd Noel, who was neither a party insider nor a communist, was acutely embarrassed. He wrote an angry letter to Bishop protesting the clumsiness of this farce, and arguing that the alleged "evidence" would be inadmissible in court.[32]

No court trial was planned; the NJM had made its point. Winston Whyte, Teddy Victor and a few others whom the regime considered dangerous were kept in prison for the rest of the PRG's four-and-a-half-year rule; the rest were released in a few months. The PRG would later regret its leniency in releasing so many; having shown itself willing to use internal terror, it could not relax its grip again without exposing itself to counter-terror.

The countdown of October-November, 1979, solidified the authority of the NJM leadership and gave it a freer hand to implement its policies. It was done, however, at the price of destroying the last traces of democracy within the society and the party, and by making violence the only vehicle for political dissent.

The *Caribbean Contact*, a respected left-leaning Catholic journal in Trinidad, doubtless spoke for many Grenadians and for Grenada's well-wishers throughout the Caribbean in a November, 1979, editorial entitled, "What Has Gone Wrong, Mr. Bishop?" Referring to its "constant, unqualified support" of the NJM and its government to date, the *Caribbean Contact* continued:

> But if that government . . . chooses, by its own actions and policies, to squander the tremendous goodwill that accompanied its rise to power, then it must not expect uncritical support for its revolution or foolishly think that all voices of dissent belong to the enemy camp.[33]

The warning was on target, but too late.

NOTES

1. "A Bright New Dawn," speech by Maurice Bishop broadcast over Radio Grenada at 10:30 a.m., March 13, 1979, reprinted in Marcus and Taber, *Maurice Bishop Speaks*, pp. 25–26.
2. Washington *Post*, September 1, 1979, page C-1.
3. *The Grenada Newsletter*, February 17, 1979, p. 2, February 24, 1979, p. 10, March 10, 1979, p. 1.
4. Conversations with Kennedy Budhlall and others; D. Sinclair DaBreo, *The Grenada Revolution* (Castries, St. Lucia: Management Advertising and Publicity Services, 1979), pp. 117–120.
5. Conversations with Kennedy Budhlall and others; DaBreo, *Grenada Revolution*, pp. 121–125.
6. DaBreo, *Grenada Revolution*, pp. 125–126; numerous conversations in Grenada.
7. "A Bright New Dawn."
8. "General Political Factors to be Considered," (typewritten MS, undated, but evidently drafted shortly after the March 13 coup) (GD unnumbered).
9. Mary Greaves, ed., "The Grenada Document: The Bitter, Epic Struggle for the Isle of Spice" (Special Publication of the *Nation* Newspaper, Bridgetown, Barbados, February 1984) p. 19. "U.S.-Grenada Relations," pp. 1–2.
10. "U.S.-Grenada Relations," pp. 1–2. "United States-Grenada Relations since the 1979 Coup" (background paper prepared for internal State Department use by Lawrence Rossin, political officer in the U.S. Embassy in Bridgetown, Barbados, late 1982), p. 44. This study, based on an exhaustive examination of diplomatic cables and other documents, as well as interviews with some of the key figures on the U.S. side, is an invaluable historical record. It provides much detail and a perspective on the U.S. perception of some critical events which hitherto have been interpreted mainly on the basis of public pronouncements by the PRG.
11. *Ibid.*, pp. 2, 4.
12. *Ibid.*, pp. 5–8; Frank Ortiz, "Grenada Before and After," letter to the editor in *The Atlantic*, vol. 253, no. 6 (June 1984), pp. 7–12.
13. "U.S.-Grenada Relations," pp. 5–18; "Declaration of the Grenada Revolution," in *Grenada: The People's Laws, 1979* (St. George's: Government Printing Office, 1980), pp. 1–4; Ortiz, "Grenada Before and After."
14. "U.S.-Grenada Relations," pp. 19–23.

15. Maurice Bishop, "In Nobody's Backyard," in Marcus and Taber, *Maurice Bishop Speaks*, pp. 26–31.
16. Handwritten notes on NJM Bureau meetings, June 22, 1974 (GD 005377), 25 July 1976 (GD unnumbered), and 16 December 1976 (GD unnumbered).
17. Handwritten notes on NJM Bureau meetings, July 22, 1976 (GD, unnumbered), and December 16, 1976 (GD, unnumbered); conversations with Kennedy Budhlall, Teddy Victor, and numerous other Grenadians.
18. "People's Law No. 19 of 1979 (Constituency Boundaries)," dated April 10, 1979, in *Grenada: The People's Laws, 1979;* conversations with Lloyd Noel, Edwin A. Heyliger (legal draftsman under the PRG) and others; "Line of March," pp. 16–17.
19. Conversations with Lloyd Noel, Edwin Heyliger, and others. People's Law No. 20 was supposed to have been the legal basis for enumerating voters in preparation for an election. However, it was never gazetted and it is missing from the bound volume of People's Laws. Allan Alexander came to St. George's while it was being drafted. He appears to have been influential in persuading Bishop to shelve the idea for a combination of legal and ideological reasons, and to proceed instead with a thorough revision of the constitution that would eventually permit the NJM to legitimize its rule without sacrificing its power.
20. "Line of March," p. 18.
21. *Ibid.*, pp. 22–23; handwritten memorandum, author unknown, conveying "some proposals arising from today's meeting," dated "May 1979" in Maurice Bishop's hand (GD 002378).
22. Conversation with Herbert Blaize; various issues of the *Torchlight* and the *Grenada Newsletter* from 1979; DaBreo, *Grenada Revolution*, pp. 200–201.
23. Interviews with Teddy Victor, Kennedy Budhlall, and others; "On Organisation, Democratisation and Code of Ethics," undated paper presented by Teddy Victor to an NJM meeting in about 1976; other miscellaneous papers and letters provided by Teddy Victor.
24. Interviews with Teddy Victor and letters provided by Victor.
25. Interviews with Teddy Victor and Kennedy Budhlall; letter from Victor to the "Prime Minister/Minister of National Security" dated July 19, 1979, provided by Victor.
26. Interviews with Winston Whyte, Teddy Victor, Kennedy Budhlall, and a leading official of the PRG security service; Situation Report to Prime Minister Bishop from the Special Branch of the Grenada

Police Service dated July 23, 1979 (GD 104259). Special Branch acted as an NJM security organ which bypassed the normal police chain of command and reported directly to the Prime Minister.

27. Alister Hughes, "PRG To Take Steps Against 'Torchlight'," *Torchlight*, September 16, 1979, p. 1; conversations with Lyden Ramdhanny and Kennedy Budhlall.

28. "Rastas to Protest," *Torchlight*, October 10, 1979, p. 1; *Grenada Newsletter*, October 20, 1979, p. 7; Sunshine, *Peaceful Rev.*, pp. 58–60; "Line of March," p. 25; conversation with Lyden Ramdhanny.

29. Catherine Sunshine, ed., *Grenada: The Peaceful Revolution* (Washington EPICA Task Force, 1982), p. 60.

30. "Pastoral Letter of Bishop Sydney A. Charles on the Ban Imposed by the People's Revolutionary Government on the 'Torchlight' Newspaper, to be Read in All Churches and Chapels on Sunday 21st October, 1979," provided by Bishop Charles.

31. *Grenada Newsletter*, October 20, 1979, pp. 11, 14; November 17, 1979, p. 1; Sunshine, *Peaceful Rev.*, pp. 66–67.

32. *Grenada Newsletter*, November 17, 1979, p. 6; conversation with Lloyd Noel.

33. *Caribbean Contact*, November 1979, p. 1.

FOUR

The People's Revolutionary Government and Its Policies

While the People's Revolutionary Government (PRG) was in power, American politicians and pundits argued over whether the Grenadian government was merely a left-wing nationalist regime or a truly communist one with dangerously close ties to the Soviets and the Cubans. When Maurice Bishop was ousted and then killed by the Coard faction—a group known for its rigid devotion to Leninist principles—many took this as proof of their belief that Bishop himself, though certainly a Marxist in some sense, was really a democratic socialist who had fallen in with a bad crowd.

The actual policies of the government, combined with the private papers of the regime, including extensive notes in Bishop's own hand, which were captured by American soldiers during the intervention, make that interpretation insupportable. There now can be no doubt that the PRG, under Bishop, set out to build socialism of a sort as close to that of the Soviet-Cuban model as could be managed in tiny Grenada.

It is not surprising that many American leaders, and perhaps most European leaders, were deceived. Most Grenadians, at least in the beginning, were deceived as well. The leaders of the New

JEWEL Movement never, in their four and a half years in power, felt safe declaring their true goals. In every important area of government policy, both foreign and domestic, the party pursued parallel policies. The public policy consisted of a deliberately difficult-to-define left-populism sprinkled with welcome social reforms. The covert policy was to build communism at home and to help spread it abroad by being of service to the Soviet bloc. By the end of 1979, Grenada was a single party dictatorship. Senior party members controlled the key positions in government. Bourgeois supporters such as Lyden Ramdhanny and Norris Bain were restricted to less sensitive positions. But, as in all communist states, the center of power was not in the government. It was in the party. And in the party, real power was exercised by a body that most Grenadians did not even know existed: the Central Committee, an elite of the fifteen to sixteen top party leaders. It set policy goals and charted the path to socialism, and it did so through careful and extremely ideological Marxist-Leninist analyses of conditions in Grenada. As in other communist regimes the executive arm of the Central Committee was the Political Bureau. It consisted of the most influential Central Committee members and was responsible for the execution of party policy. It was assisted by an Economic Bureau and by Bernard Coard's Organizing Committee.

In the day-to-day operations of the party, Coard's Organizing Committee held the reins. It was responsible for party discipline and for overseeing the work of lower organs, including the National Youth Organization and the "Parish Coordinating Bodies." The Parish Coordinating Bodies in turn supervised the local "organizations of popular democracy": parish councils, zonal councils, village councils—the ultimate incarnations of the Assemblies of the People foreseen in the 1973 NJM manifesto. But where the NJM manifesto had promised a system of direct democracy, in which power would flow from the bottom up, the system established in 1979 became an instrument for controlling the people from the top down.

The ideological justification for this system was the backwardness of Grenadian society: the low political consciousness of the Grenadian masses, their lack of education, their long history of political and economic suppression, and their poverty and primitive living conditions. The self-appointed task of the "vanguard party" was to reverse these conditions as quickly as possible, liberating the working masses from poverty and ignorance so they could intelligently manage their own affairs. The means to this end was the "dictatorship of the proletariat" exercised by the party in the interest of all working people.

It was, in its way, a noble conception. And the NJM, at the start, pursued it with energy and determination. The result was an almost total failure. The NJM lacked money, matériel, personnel, and expertise. It was consistently confounded by its ideology and its insistence on managing from the top. More importantly, the party lost the collaboration of the people. As the euphoria of the first days of the revolution gave way to gathering popular resentment at being manipulated, this loss of popular support became the most serious problem of all.

THE SOCIAL PROGRAM

The NJM did its best work in areas least susceptible to ideological distortions. Social conditions in Grenada—health, nutrition, housing, education—were awful, at least for many of the people. And the problems (e.g., primitive hygiene) were so basic that a few simple, and reasonably obvious, reforms could hardly fail to improve things. What was needed was energy, and in the beginning the NJM had that. Eventually, even the social programs were destroyed by party bickering, bad management, ideological quarrels, and foreign interference, but the NJM made an honest start.

The PRG's health program is a good example. It started with the sound insight that a poor country like Grenada could make more progress by undertaking preventive medicine programs than by trying, vainly, to finance fantastically expensive medical technology or a sophisticated health care establishment. The government set about instead to prevent disease by inculcating sound hygienic procedures and cleaning up obvious sources of infection. Since preventive medicine aimed at improving the basic health of all the people and at shifting resources away from big hospitals and into the communities, it was also portrayed as part of the broader struggle for social justice and democracy.[1]

Public health officials organized films, lectures, and workshops on preventive medicine for groups. The Parish Coordinating Bodies and the local chapters of the National Youth Organization and the National Women's Organization reached individuals through house-to-house visits and posters. They encouraged people to clean up garbage, eliminate mosquito breeding areas, get immunizations and take advantage of local public health facilities. Beginning in 1981 with a pilot project in St. David's, the PRG set about establishing a District Health Team in each parish. It also increased the number of local health clinics and made an effort, at least, to repair or rebuild those that had become dilapidated under Gairy. The Ministry of Agriculture set up a Food and Nutrition Council to oversee a school lunch program and the distribution of free milk (donated by the European Economic Community) to needy children. (Both programs were plagued by irregular service and minor corruption.) The water supply and sewage treatment got special attention.[2]

The government also tried to regularize fees at the General Hospital in St. George's. Physicians were forbidden to see private patients in the hospital, though they could still see private patients in town. At the hospital all patients were admitted by the administration rather than by the doctors, and all were given free care. Free care had been available to the poor previously, but the intent of the new system was to standardize care and prevent discrimination against poor patients.[3] Eventually, however, conditions at the hospital deteriorated badly.

Medical services could not have been so expanded, especially in the countryside, without help from abroad. Money came from Europe, CARICOM, Latin America, the U.S., and the Soviet bloc. But it was the Cuban medical brigade that got the most attention and had the biggest impact.[4] The brigade first arrived in June, 1979, three months after the coup, with seven doctors, three dentists, a radiographer and a coordinator. Eventually the number of doctors more than doubled. The brigade did some good, but less than it might have, had its purposes been purely medical rather than partly ideological and propagandistic as they were.

The Cubans provided specialist services such as ophthamology and orthopedics, and all but introduced dental care to Grenada. They also helped bring health services to remote areas, particularly the smaller island of Carriacou. Independent observers studying the medical situation in late 1979 noted that the Cubans worked hard and had created a generally favorable impression. "The volume of patients they have seen has been well publicized. . . . " The very same observers, however, noted that the quality of the Cuban medical work was difficult to assess, especially because Grenadians avoided comment on the subject. The Cubans seemed unwilling or unable to collaborate with Grenadian medical personnel. They kept to themselves and made no effort to train indigenous health professionals. Rather they concentrated "on showing that their system is more 'productive' than the existing system in Grenada."[5]

That attitude, combined with the publicity and other benefits the Cubans received, alienated Grenadian physicians. The Grenadian doctors also had doubts about the qualifications of young, and perhaps inexperienced, Cuban doctors placed in positions of authority. One Grenadian physician observed that a few good physicians had come with the first Cuban team, but that these had soon departed and were replaced with inferior practitioners. The Grenadian people were lukewarm about the Cuban doctors. Several months after the fall of the PRG an American political scientist polling Grenadian opinion found that 78 percent of the people he polled could think of nothing they missed about the Cuban presence in Grenada. Only 1 percent mentioned the departed Cuban doctors.[6]

On balance, despite good intentions and foreign resources, little progress was made, and some things got worse. The commonsensical campaign for hygiene and sanitation was very useful. And the increased number of local medical clinics made care more available, especially in the countryside. But all the more technically demanding aspects of health care either stayed bad or got worse: the NJM people were bad managers and, even worse, insisted on managing areas in which they had no expertise.

Drugs were always in short supply, despite free shipments from Cuba and Eastern Europe. Grenadian medical personnel remained as underpaid and demoralized as they had been before the revolution. Conditions in the public hospitals were deplorable. Even party loyalist and ideological hardliner Phyllis Coard (Bernard's wife) wrote an angry letter to the Political Bureau pointing out the horrible mismanagement of the PRG health authorities. According to the letter, the medical practices resulted in "*many, many,* unnecessary deaths occurring within 48 hours of surgery," and the failure to improve "appalling" conditions at the mental hospital. In June 1982, a foreign doctor with extensive worldwide experience wrote an angry personal letter to Bishop complaining that conditions had actually deteriorated during her six months of service in a senior position in the General Hospital. "Services are crumbling. . . . we have an unnecessary death every week."[7]

Similar problems appeared in another much-vaunted program: the campaign to repair dilapidated schools and housing. The campaign was certainly necessary: in 1980, 45 percent of Grenadians rated their own housing as "bad." Many houses were little more than rotting wooden shacks without electricity or running water. Drawing largely on funds from OPEC, the government began granting housing loans of up to $1,000 per household at repayment terms of as little as $5 per month. Former PRG officials claim that over 5,000 homes were repaired by 1983. But reports of widespread corruption cast doubt on the government's figures. Allegedly some NJM supporters used this fund to accumulate "little lumber yards underneath their houses." Political favoritism often directed the loans not to those who needed them but to those whom the NJM needed. Under the NJM, as under Gairy, Grenada owed most of its new housing construction to remittances from Grenadians working abroad in England, the United States, or Canada.[8]

The government also launched a massive school repair campaign. It started by organizing voluntary weekend work brigades to make repairs in community schools with materials supplied by the government. The work brigades were enthusiastic in the beginning, and made some minor repairs. But they were not equal to the task of major renovations. The government itself tried to take up the slack, but once again shortages of money, expertise, and management ability destroyed the program. Government school buildings deteriorated under the NJM and some had to be abandoned.[9]

Among the social programs, education itself was the NJM's top priority—and its biggest failure. For, unlike the public health and hygiene campaign, education presented all sorts of opportunities for ideological vandalism. In an opening address to the National Education Conference on July 2, 1979, Maurice Bishop laid out the regime's educational philosophy. "Perhaps the worst crime that colonialism left our country . . . is the education system." That system, he proclaimed, had been developed to strip the colonized people of their own history, culture, and values, to stifle their creativity, and to perpetuate class privilege. The aim of the PRG's educational policy would be to liberate the mass of people from ignorance and a sense of cultural inferiority and to democratize Grenadian society: "We must use the educational system and process as a means of preparing the new man for the new life in the new society we are trying to build."[10]

Because education was for everyone, young and old, one of the first and most important targets was adult illiteracy, which by NJM accounts was running at more than 30 percent. Under the slogan "each one teach one," the government's new Center for Popular Education set out to mobilize volunteer tutors to fight illiteracy. The goal was to bring approximately a third of Grenada's illiterate adults to basic literacy within six months, by February 1981. It was one of the government's most popular programs, and it seems to have achieved its first goal. In any event 881 people received certificates at the completion of the course.[11]

The CPE's first success was its last. The program lost steam, fewer students registered, more dropped out. Ideology in the program itself was part of the problem. Some students were put off by the political messages that crept into CPE instructional materials and by the increasingly obvious pressures the PRG used to recruit new registrants. Others were upset by the disrespectful and condescending manner of their tutors. But the essential difficulty was that by 1982 most Grenadians were either hostile to the revolution or disillusioned with it. The PRG could no longer whip up enthusiasm for voluntary campaigns. In 1982, Minister of Education Jacqueline Creft tried to revitalize the program. But by that time, according to one former member of the CPE's advisory committee, "nothing they touched seemed to work."[12]

Another program that went aground on the shoals of ideology was the National In-Service Teacher Education Program (NISTEP). Again the need was real: 70 percent of Grenada's teachers had no professional training of any kind, and every year many of the country's best qualified teachers emigrated or dropped out of the profession.

The NJM decided to kill two birds with one stone. Under the NISTEP plan, worked out in collaboration with the University of the West Indies School of Education and the ever-present Cuban advisors, teachers would conduct classes four days a week and attend training sessions the fifth. The in-service training would last three years.[13] Meanwhile, on the days their teachers were away at training, the students would be turned over to the Community-School Day Program (CSDP), which featured field trips à la revolution. The idea here was that the children should acquire a greater respect for the work of the proletariat and that the community should play a bigger part in educating the children. So the children would go on trips to, say, a banana-packing plant or a brick factory, learn about the work done there, and even participate in it. An official report explained: "Exposure to this range of skills at such an early age obviously facilitates the students' choices of careers later in life, as much as it also enables them to understand more fully their own roles in nation building and the revolution."[14]

Neither program really worked. Many NISTEP instructors were radicals who had few hesitations about bringing their politics into the classroom. The dropout rate was high, at least partly because the teacher trainees resented the radicalism of the instructors. In fact politicization became a problem for teachers across the board. Teachers at some schools were harassed, transferred or even dismissed for their political views. One economics teacher at the Institute for Further Education who refused to teach Marxist economics was harassed into resigning. Grenadians worried about the large numbers of Cubans and other Caribbean leftists working in the island's educational system, and were really alarmed when Soviet teachers began to arrive in 1983.[15] And, after all was said and done, teacher emigration actually increased during the NJM regime.

At the Community-School Development Program, the first problem to show up was the difficulty of finding field trips or speakers interesting enough to hold the children's attention for one day a week. Truancy was rampant on CSDP days. This too was part of a larger problem. In addition to time lost to CSDP, more time was lost and classes were repeatedly disrupted when children were called out for the rallies, drills, and mobilizations of the militia, the National Youth Organization, the Young Pioneers, the student councils and other revolutionary organizations. Moreover, the ideology inculcated by the NJM through these groups undermined discipline both at home and in school. Parents were dismayed by children who rejected their authority and became gun-toting revolutionaries, drunk with the rhetoric of violence. Principals and teachers had trouble maintaining order in classrooms. A boy at one school pulled a gun on a teacher. The situation grew so serious that the PRG itself became concerned: Minister of Education Creft formed a committee of teachers and principals to draw up a code of school discipline.[16]

Creft, who eventually became Bishop's mistress, was a former convent schoolgirl. Though she was an NJM member and at times sounded like a devout revolutionary, in truth she was torn between Catholicism and communism. That ambivalence, which she never resolved, had a moderating effect. But as time passed, her power in her own ministry began to wane. More-aggressive Leninists, including Phyllis Coard, Bernard Coard's wife, pushed for more radical, and eventually more repressive, education policies. The radicals' most important goal was to reduce the influence of the churches over education, replacing religious belief (always strong in Grenada) with Marxist doctrine. Early on, Wesley College was removed from the control of the Methodist Church. Some Grenadians feared that this would set a precedent for nationalizing all religious schools, which would mean 74 percent of the schools in the country. Somewhat later, religious instruction was removed from its traditional place in the school curriculum, to the consternation of most parents and teachers.

By the fall of 1983, a real crackdown, long feared, finally began. With Cuban help, the government moved to standardize textbooks and to introduce Marxist political education (labeled civics) directly into the curriculum. The party had decided it was time to replace "reactionary and redundant elements" with "democratic and progressive elements" better suited to inculcating proper political views. The PRG suddenly transferred 18 principals and teachers out of their schools without consulting the mainly church-affiliated school boards. All remaining principals were summoned to a five-hour meeting at which a new "Principals Council" was founded, as a means of supervising their political orientation.[17] Fortunately, the collapse of the PRG interrupted this campaign of repression and intimidation before it was fully developed.

By one measure, education probably managed to just about hold its own during the four and one half years of NJM rule. The CPE and NISTEP programs had some successes; on the other hand, teacher emigration increased and classroom disruptions and lost teaching-time hurt.

THE ECONOMIC PROGRAM
I: REVOLUTIONARY CONTROL

As in every other policy area, the NJM's economic policy had two agendas: one for public consumption, the other known only to party insiders. But the public plan and the secret plan were not entirely contradictory. Rather, the public plan consisted of the first cautious steps on the way to a far more radical vision: socialism on an explicitly Soviet model.

The model toward which the PRG claimed to be striving and

toward which it actually was striving in the near-term was a "mixed economy, state sector dominant."[18] Radical proposals such as those of the 1973 NJM manifesto were postponed, partly because the proposals would have been unpopular, partly because the government could not yet afford to pursue them and still needed a reasonably healthy private sector. The program, as publicly set out, was an apparently rational, if fairly ambitious, plan for reform through economic diversification under strong government leadership, leading to a modernized, more industrialized economy. Thus, for instance, the government fulfilled a longstanding NJM promise to promote domestic processing of Grenada's produce by setting up the state-owned Agro-Industries, Ltd., to do just that. It also created a National Fisheries Corporation to rationalize and improve the harvesting of fish for domestic consumption. Gairy's nightclubs were confiscated by the government to form the basis of the state-owned Grenada Resorts Corporation, through which the government hoped to influence and expand the tourist industry. In 1983 the corporation purchased the former Holiday Inn, by far the largest hotel on the island.

One of the government's most aggressive moves was into banking. It inherited one government bank from the Gairy regime and started two more. Their main function was to finance the PRG's extremely ambitious capital improvement projects. In its first year the government doubled Gairy's capital budget to $16 million and increased it further from there. The money went to road reconstruction (including rural feeder roads over which delicate crops had to be shipped), a port expansion project, Grenada's first public transportation project and, of course, the International Airport at Point Salines. Apart from the contribution of the state-owned banks, these projects were funded mostly by foreign loans and grants, largely from Western sources.

The government did place some restrictions on the big import-export firms that had traditionally handled most of Grenada's foreign trade. Through its Marketing and National Imports Board (MNIB). It monopolized the import of rice, sugar, powdered milk and cement. It imposed a licensing requirement on all imports and exports (which allowed the government to monitor prices) and established some profit ceilings. On the other hand, the government tried to promote private investment in tourism, light manufacturing, and infrastructure development. And it made a policy of encouraging small and medium sized business ventures.[19] The government also encouraged cooperatives in farming, fishing, crafts and light industry, which it saw as a potential third sector of the economy between the public and private sectors.[20]

This was the public program. It consisted largely of a plan to modernize and industrialize the Grenadian economy. But it was part and parcel of the secret program, known only to the inner circle of the party, the goal of which was the establishment of socialism on the Soviet model through the gradual development of state capitalism and the collectivization of agriculture. Modernizing the economy was essential to building socialism, which could only rest on an industrial economy. As Bishop explained in classic Marxist terminology, "it is, as we know, the objective material basis of the economy that determines and directs the political, social and cultural development of the society as a whole." This objective basis was not present in Grenada because it had "a backward undeveloped economy, with a . . . primitive level of technological and economic development," and "a low level of development of the productive forces," which "resulted in very underdeveloped class formations."

But building a modern economy had its dangers, as Bishop pointed out in his 1982 "Line of March" speech. Typically his explanation drew on Soviet experience:

> . . . if we are not careful capitalism rather than socialism will be the end product, just like when Lenin had formulated NEP right after the Great October Socialist Revolution, the Bolsheviks too had that same problem and concern.
>
> Simultaneously we will be nurturing the shoots of capitalism and the shoots of socialism and the question is . . . how you . . . ensure that socialism is what comes out and not capitalism. We have the same problem as the young Soviet State faced but a million times more difficult, because our state sector is much smaller . . . And of course we have a much smaller and less ideologically developed working class . . . In other words comrades, we have a tightrope that we have to monitor very carefully as we walk it—*every single day* . . .

What this means is that our primary task must be to sink the ideas of Marxism/Leninism amongst the working people so that their own ideological level can advance . . .[21]

The details of the secret program were worked out in an ideological study group established within the Central Committee. Maurice Bishop's extensive notes covering the meetings of this group from 1980 to 1983 have survived.

The group followed a fixed methodology. First, along with some theoretical texts, it would study the historical development of the Soviet Union at different stages of its development. A theoretical discussion followed, designed to distill the essential points to be learned from the Soviet experience. Finally, in a segment entitled "creative application," the party leaders discussed how to adapt the lessons they had learned to Grenadian conditions in order to move the revolution ahead along Soviet lines.

On the basis of this study, the Central Committee members concluded, as Bishop mentioned in his "Line of March" speech later, that Grenada was in a condition similar to that of the Soviet Union in the early 1920s when Lenin instituted the New Economic Program. The revolutionary regime needed to make a temporary tactical accommodation with the capitalist producers so it could consolidate itself and prepare the next steps in the class struggle. But eventually, in careful stages, the regime would move to undermine and eliminate the exploiting classes, neutralize the petty bourgeoisie (including the more well-to-do peasants) and shift power to the working class—that is, to the vanguard party itself. Grenada, the leaders noted, had one unique problem that the Soviets hadn't faced: it had no industrial proletariat to speak of. Therefore, the leaders decided, for the time being youth would play the leadership role in this revolution, and youth would have to be educated to a proletarian point of view.[22]

But there was another problem. There wasn't much of a rural proletariat either. The bulk of Grenada's poorer people were either small independent farmers or rural workers. And even many of the rural workers, most of whom worked for wages on larger farms, also owned their own tiny plots and were fiercely attached to them. The NJM was about to wage a class war on behalf of a class that did not exist in order to build a workers' state in a country in which, at least in the Marxist sense, there were few workers.

The solution was to make more workers. That was the goal of industrialization. But in rural Grenada it would also be the goal of the NJM's agricultural policies. The near-term plan was set forth by Bernard Coard in early 1980: All estates over 100 acres (about 30 percent of the 40,000 acres of farm land in Grenada) would become state collective farms. All "peasants' lands" (about 50 percent of the total) would become cooperatives. The remaining 20 percent—lands not currently under cultivation— would be divided between state farms and cooperatives. Eventually even the peasants' cooperatives would be fully collectivized: no peasant would own his own plot, no matter how small; and all agricultural work would be done by landless "workers."

Bishop wrote: "In a P.B. [petty-bourgeois] society such as Russia was in 1917, the transition from capitalism to socialism can only be effected by moving away from small-scale individual peasant farming through the development of state farming and socialized cooperative farming." Ewart Layne summarized the party's position thus: "The only way to transform the country-side along soc[ialist] lines . . . is through the radical restruc[turing] of [the] countryside on [the] basis of collectivisation and state farms."[23]

In effect, the party hoped to build a proletarian revolution by proletarianizing agriculture. Bishop noted that to build socialism, it is "necessary to abolish the difference between factory workers and peasants and make workers out of all of them." For the time being, the party would have to focus on the first steps of the process: eliminating the large landowners and founding coopera-tives as the best economic form to promote socialism "in this historical period." But the aim of the cooperative movement, Bishop wrote, "is to kill individualism."[24]

This "land reform" plan, as it was publicly called, was per-haps the most striking example of the NJM's slavish adherence to its conception of Marxist-Leninist orthodoxy, in total disregard of the actual wishes and needs of the Grenadian people. There was no real land hunger in Grenada, nor were there any deep-rooted class antagonisms. After the explosion of 1951, which resulted from resentments over specific grievances, the peasants had been happy to go back to their traditional relationship with the planters. Moreover, the planter-class itself was gradually dying out and the plantations were breaking up, largely because large-scale agriculture was unprofitable in Grenada. The rugged landscape of the island lent itself more to small-scale, intensive cultivation of tree crops such as nutmeg, cocoa, and fruits. For this as well as for other, historical reasons, Grenada had developed the strongest small-peasant agriculture in the eastern Caribbean, a region where the ownership of land was "the center of gravity, the linchpin of a syndrome of values best characterized as conservative."[25]

Nevertheless, as early as 1980, the NJM began to prepare a sweeping land reform. Party leaders debated but rejected outright confiscation, which, in conservative Grenada, would certainly have provoked a fierce reaction. Purchase or seizure with subsequent compensation would be expensive and could involve lengthy and acrimonious negotiations. Finally, the leadership hit on the solution of mandatory leasing, and incorporated it into law as the Land Development and Utilization Law of 1981. The leases were fictions: though actual lease agreements were drawn up, no rent was ever paid. But the fiction fit in with the public relations strategy precluding any mention of actual "acquisition" of the land: "Much careful analysis has gone into this area to ensure that . . . when the bourgeoisie respond as they must, they will not be able to arouse panic reaction among the peasantry and other small-commodity owners." According to another fiction, all land seized was identified as idle or under-utilized.

The leasing law would be used to seize all estates over 50 acres, but in two stages. Those over 100 acres would be subject to seizure immediately. Those between 50 and 100 would be seized five or 10 years later. The new law would also provide opportunities for political punishment since "approximately 90 percent of those hostile to the revolution" could lose their land under the law.[26]

Landowners were characterized by class, along strict Leninist lines. Peasants with one acre or less were designated as "poor peasants," those with two to six acres as "middle peasants." In slavish imitation of the Russian experience, peasants with seven to 50 acres were designated as "kulaks." Those with 50 to 100 acres were middle capitalists, and above 100 acres was the "large capitalist" plantocracy. Once characterized, their fates were clear. Large and middle capitalists would be eliminated entirely, though some who collaborated with the regime would be kept on for a while. The "kulaks," according to the Soviet model, would have to be crushed. Middle peasants would be embraced as allies, and the poor peasants and landless rural workers would be supported.[27]

By 1982, land reform had begun to gather momentum. The Land Development and Utilization Law was streamlined to allow the government to bypass legal formalities and move to immediate seizure when the "Minister in his discretion" deemed the national interest to be involved. The government compiled long lists of estates subject to compulsory lease, complete with notations on the acreage and number of workers, as well as on the politics of the estate owners. The USSR provided advice and support including a shipment of tractors. By July 1983, a total of 9,000 acres had been seized, and the Central Committee was already discussing the next phase of the operation—the seizure of estates between 50 and 100 acres.[28]

By that time the government was also planning to institute a compulsory national labor service to procure young workers for the collectivized farms. The Land Reform Committee was "agreed that this is the only approach that will bring and keep large numbers of youth in agriculture." This forced-labor program, which the government expected to be fiercely resisted, was to have been announced by Bishop during the fifth anniversary of the revolution in March 1984. The Commander in Chief would justify the move as necessary to defend the revolution "against the permanent enemy, imperialism."[29]

While the land reform was unfolding, the PRG was busy developing other mechanisms for controlling the economy. One mechanism was the trade union movement. As a Marxist "vanguard" party, the NJM regarded trade unions as an adjunct to its own efforts to seize and hold power for the working class. Before the vanguard party seized power, the unions' job was to help bring down the capitalist state. Afterwards their job was to support the workers' government, help secure its power within the economy and strengthen the economy itself by increasing production. For example, after the revolution the NJM tried to get the unions to help administer a productivity campaign, monitoring every worker "hour by hour" for evidence of poor or praiseworthy work habits, and sponsoring production competitions.[30] (One of these productivity campaigns produced Grenada's own Stakhanov, a worker called Coonyar who was immortalized for inventing a beetle trap.)

As in any communist state, a conflict of interest emerged. The revolution was, in theory, for the workers. But the revolutionary government, though it might sincerely wish to improve the lot of the workers, had other concerns as well, such as balancing the budget and keeping the economy afloat. It as often found itself disciplining the workers as advancing them. In Grenada, as in all communist countries, the conflict was most painfully obvious in state-owned enterprises. In these the government itself was the employer facing the workers across the bargaining table. It is such situations that make communist governments insist on controlling the unions. The workers cannot be allowed to organize against the workers' state.

The PRG never managed to control all the unions, and in the opening months of the revolution it actually lost ground in some unions in which the NJM had once had significant influence. By 1980, the government had its first serious confrontation with labor. The public service workers represented by the Public Workers' Union, the Grenada Union of Teachers, and the Technical and Allied Workers' Union, demanded a 60 percent wage increase for 1980. The three unions had felt cheated by their 1978 settlement with Gairy. At that time the NJM had supported them and the unions were now hoping to take advantage of the "revolutionary situation" to make up lost ground.

They were disappointed immediately. It was several months before the PRG even agreed to negotiate, and even then the government offered a much smaller settlement. In its own defense, the PRG began a propaganda campaign explaining that money was short because "the big imperialist countries" were squeezing the poor countries economically. Under such conditions, it proclaimed, large wage settlements were against the national interest.[31]

In late February 1981 the unions concluded that the government was bargaining in bad faith and agreed on a one-day sickout. It was only partly successful. Jim Wardally of the Technical and Allied Workers' Union (one of the NJM members who had been arrested in 1979 in Washington for gun-running) persuaded his workers not to stay out. A PRG propaganda campaign laced with warnings of "very firm action" intimidated others. And when the PRG did in fact suspend some workers who honored the sickout, the unions caved in and accepted the government's best offer.

Still, for the PRG, the whole incident was a nasty shock. The leadership reacted with typical paranoia. A secret Political Bureau resolution detected in the sickout "a definite plot by reactionary, opportunist, and counter-revolutionary elements" with "definite evidence . . . of CIA involvement."[32] The incident strengthened the leaders' resolve to bring the unions under party control. Using a combined program of infiltration, activism, and intimidation they eventually succeeded. By the end of its rule, the NJM had a firm grip on all but three of the independent unions: the Seamen's and Waterfront Workers' Union, the Public Workers' Union, and the taxi drivers' union. The unions founded by the NJM remained firmly in party hands. The agricultural unions were always solidly under the regime's control. A 1982 report listed the Agricultural and General Workers' Union's (AGWU) two main goals as the recruitment of workers into the party and into the mass organizations associated with the party. But, partly because it was so subservient, the AGWU was never much use to the regime.[33]

ECONOMIC PROGRAM
II: BOTTOM LINE VS. PARTY LINE

The PRG did not want to eliminate Grenada's private economy, at least not immediately, but to subordinate it to the state. Because, in the view of party leaders, the political essence of socialism was the dictatorship of the proletariat, its economic essence was large-scale industrialization. And to build industry the PRG needed the resources and expertise of Grenada's entrepreneurs. At the same time, the whole point of the revolution was to give the "working class" control of the society, including the economy. One tool would be a strong state sector. But the most important device was to be central planning. Through central planning, the government hoped that it could continue to draw on the skills of more-or-less private entrepreneurs while retaining a firm grip on the economy as a whole. It was to be a compromise between a foolish and extreme attempt to run every detail of the economy and a negligent policy of allowing the capitalists so much power as to effectively betray the revolution. It didn't work. The compromise turned into a contradiction between the overt, pragmatic goals of the regime and its hidden ideological agenda.

That contradiction was epitomized in the contrasting personalities and policy recommendations of the PRG's two economic luminaries: Finance Minister Bernard Coard, the party's chief Marxist-Leninist theoretician, and millionaire Lyden Ramdhanny, its Minister of Tourism and most prominent and powerful capitalist fellow-traveler. Coard, the tough administrator of economic policy, was first and foremost a man of doctrinaire principle. He recognized the hardships caused by the PRG's headlong pursuit of industrial development and social transformation. But he was also convinced that only radical social and economic restructuring could create in Grenada the material and political conditions within which a class conscious proletariat could develop. Coard was an open Stalinist, and he was willing to pay the price for socialism.

Ramdhanny, a slight and soft-spoken businessman, left-wing but not a communist, was the voice of pragmatism within the PRG. He agreed with the party's policies, at least as he understood them from his own more moderate socialist perspective. But he urged caution, patience, a minimum of rhetoric, and wherever possible, persuasion. He agreed in principle, for instance, with the land reform program and helped implement it. But he questioned whether the government yet had the expertise to run a number of large state farms efficiently. He supported the decision to control profits, but opposed extending government control too far because he feared it would discourage private initiative and hurt the economy. He advocated state planning as a long-term goal, but argued for using scarce technical personnel first and foremost to solve the PRG's more urgent practical problems.[34]

Under the NJM regime, however, the real power was in the hands of the Marxist-Leninist insiders, which, in economic affairs, meant Coard and his colleagues. And they were more than a little ambivalent about the likes of Lyden Ramdhanny. Party leaders told themselves repeatedly that they needed such bourgeois allies. But they worried constantly about the dangers of counter-revolution or resurgent capitalist power, and suspected the capitalists of treachery at every turn. In the 1982 statement of the party's "Line of March," Bishop defended the theory of class alliance. But then he went on to reassure his party colleagues that the bourgeoisie had been stripped of any real power or rights:

> ... when we want to hold Zonal Councils and we don't want them there, we keep them out. When they want to put out a newspaper and we don't want that, we close it down. When they want freedom of expression to attack the Government ... we crush them and jail them. They are not part of the dictatorship ... They have lost some of the rights they used to have. Now it is the working people who have these rights, not the bourgeoisie. ... That is ... what dictatorship or rule means.[35]

These attitudes were no secret from the entrepreneurs. They knew what was being taught in the NJM's worker education sessions about exploiting and exploited classes, and the implications for them. Nor were the young ministers of the PRG reluctant to bare the mailed fist at even a slight provocation. The *Torchlight* incident proved that early, as did the seizure of a Coca-Cola plant over a minor labor dispute. Other incidents followed. Such things worried the island's businessmen. They worried also about the sharp falloff in tourism resulting from the

Central America and the Caribbean

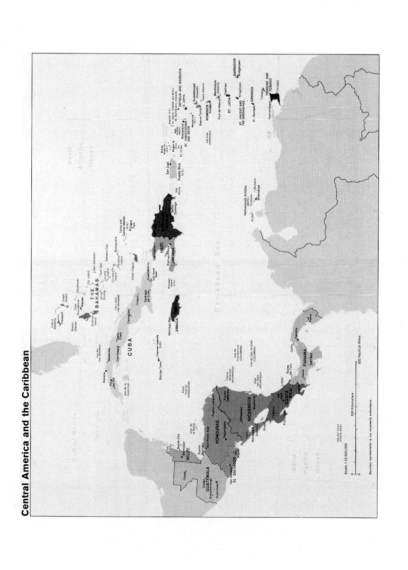

Saint Georges-Point Salines Peninsula

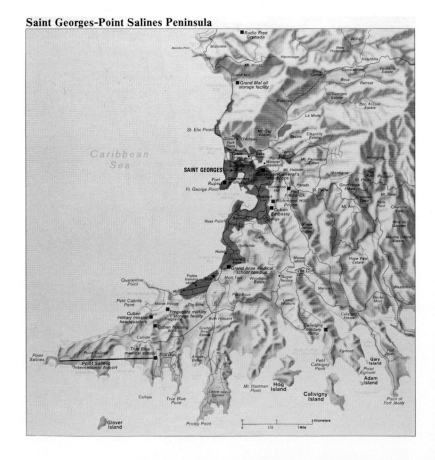

Maurice Bishop (far left) leading his father's funeral procession. Rupert Bishop was killed in the 1973–74 disturbances over Grenadian independence.

Men, women, and children marching in Hero's Day parade, June 19th (year uncertain).

A "route march" to defend against one of many phantom invasions (date unknown).

PRA drawn up in front of wall at Fort Rupert where Bishop and others were later shot.

Bishop reviewing troops at Fort Rupert (Fort George), where he was eventually murdered.

Left to right: Selwyn Strachen, Terrence Moore, unknown, Maurice Bishop, Kenrick Radix, Unison Whiteman.

Lyden Ramdhanny and Kenrick Radix.

Bernard Coard

Crowd waiting for Bishop at Market Square, St. George's on October 19, 1983. Note sign on truck "We want Bishop/ No Coard/Down with Communism." Most Grenadians never knew that Bishop was a communist.

Bishop (in center of photo, with crooked elbow) being taken by the crowd from his house arrest, October 19, 1983.

Post-PRG graffiti in St. George's.

Post-PRG graffiti in West Indian patois. It means, "JEWEL kills our children."

government's radical anti-American rhetoric. They worried about the decline in labor discipline, which the NJM's policies encouraged. They worried about the government's creeping encroachment into the import-export trade, which merchants saw as a prelude to their eventual expropriation or bankruptcy. Because of these and other worries, within a relatively short time business confidence collapsed and private investment began to dry up. Those businessmen who did not flee the country—and many did—settled in for a bitter siege.

A similar situation prevailed on private farms: agricultural laborers influenced by AGWU agitation expected a day's pay for as little as four hours' work. Unable to make a profit (especially with nutmeg prices low), and fearing possible government seizure of their lands in the long run, the farmers stopped investing in fertilizer and equipment, and production began to drop.

While the private sector was being demoralized, the public sector was being overextended. Though government enterprises and construction projects led to a favorable growth rate on paper, the enterprises performed poorly and construction bogged down after the first year or two. Some of the problems were the same affecting private business: labor discipline declined and workers were constantly interrupted for rallies, ideological training sessions and militia drills. But in addition, state enterprises had to contend with political cronyism. The NJM repeatedly placed supporters in influential positions for which they were not qualified. Because the party leaders were in a rush, many favorite projects were poorly thought-out; and money, material, and technical skills were lacking everywhere.[36]

Agro-Industries for example, a long-standing NJM priority, wasn't properly organized until 1981 and lost $202,524 (Eastern Caribbean dollars) that year. It came close to breaking even in 1982, but it was plagued with shortages and equipment failures. The National Fisheries were referred to as a "disaster area" in party meetings. The cement-hulled boats provided by the Cubans were inefficient and broke down constantly. Out of a fleet of 11, only three were still operating by October 1982. Poor management and the disaffection of Grenadian fishermen led to an almost total breakdown of the project. By 1982 the PRG had been forced to pump in EC$350,000 to compensate for financial losses and was preparing to close down the company. Grenada Farms Corporation, which managed the state farms, showed a loss of EC$640,000 in 1981, and in 1982 it was in the red by EC$1.5 million. Workers on the state farms, according to confidential reports, were doing little if any work after lunchtime and were producing only about a third of their wages. The cooperative farms were even worse off. Most were amateur operations that soon fell victim to internal bickering. In fact only one farming co-op survived the demise of the PRG; it antedated the NJM regime, and its members were out of sympathy with the regime.[37]

The list went on. By 1982 only the government-owned utilities (electricity, telephone, and water), the Port Authority, and the Marketing and National Imports Board were showing significant profits. And that was not because of any improvement in their operations, but because the PRG steadily increased rates, taxes, and custom duties as well as the prices of monopolized items. The economy was still further burdened by government extravagances. NJM leaders, ever conscious of security, travelled about the country in caravans of cars with heavy military escorts. Grenada sent large deputations to numerous international meetings and on tours of foreign countries, often for purely ideological purposes. Numerous foreign visitors and "advisors" also came to Grenada to participate in major celebrations or to help in the progress of the revolution. Most of these visitors were subsidized in some way by the government. The Ministry for National Mobilization and the ideological departments of other ministries tapped government funds for political purposes, often giving little or no account of the money. And of course there was the huge burden of supporting the People's Revolutionary Army.

To all of this was added a world recession in 1980–82, a drop in demand for Grenada's agricultural products, bad weather, and crop diseases. The government deficit, which stood at 3.3 percent of gross domestic product in 1978, rose to 16.1 percent in 1979 and 32.3 percent by 1982, and continued climbing. Cash-flow problems mounted and reached crisis proportions by 1983. For the first few years the PRG had managed to forestall the consequences of the deficits. In 1979 it found extra money by cleaning up some of the corruption and waste of Gairy's government. In 1980, aid from OPEC countries, including Syria, Iraq, Libya, and Algeria helped. In 1981 the government secured a loan from the International Monetary Fund. By 1982, though, the PRG had to turn inward. A spate of legislation was passed. Taxes and duties were raised, further pinching the economy. And, in an even more drastic move, all banks were required to deposit 20 percent of their funds with the government.[38]

In the opinion of one senior bank manager, the new deposit law represented "the beginning of the end" for the economy. The requirement drained all remaining liquidity from the economy, and investment virtually ceased. At around the same time, the government's cash flow crisis dried up funds for capital improvement projects already underway and led to major layoffs. The only exception to this rule was the international airport project. The airport had constantly absorbed 40 to 50 percent of capital investment funds. Now, despite the condition of the economy, the government diverted money and supplies from every possible source in order to complete the airport in time for the fifth anniversary of the revolution in March 1984.[39]

In April 1983, Finance Minister Coard had to inform his colleagues that the government was in desperate financial straits and was facing even harder times ahead. The only hope seemed to be another loan from the IMF, a prospect the PRG pursued with desperate energy. But the IMF announced that it would impose strict conditions, and the government despaired of meeting them. In a leadership meeting on August 3, 1983, Bishop suggested "that we use the Suriname and Cuban experience in keeping two sets of records in the banks" to help fudge the liquidity problem. A followup meeting on August 10 confirmed this decision and discussed seeking "technical assistance . . . from Cuba and Nicaragua" to help the government cook its books.[40]

In sum, by autumn 1983, the economy over which Bernard Coard presided was at the point of collapse. It was, to use the words of a prominent Grenadian businessman, "overextended, overborrowed, and overtaxed" and the government had to resort to financial chicanery to keep its head above water. The state of the economy certainly contributed to the self-destruction of the PRG. Had the regime survived, it probably would have had to resort to ever more draconian economic measures. Already the signs of such a development were on the horizon: During an August 1983 Political Bureau meeting, it was suggested that Coard "read the riot act" to private investors who had declined to invest in a government-owned hotel, and that he "get them to make specific commitments on the issue." As it was, the PRG left behind an unfinanced deficit of EC$7 million as its legacy to Grenada's future government.[41]

FOREIGN POLICY

The foreign policy of the People's Revolutionary Government revolved around two poles: ideology and aid. There was an inter-relationship between the two in that the NJM's ideology led it to look to Cuba and the Soviet bloc as the main source of support for its regime. The NJM leaders seem to have been genuinely persuaded that communist countries had a greater concern than the West for the plight of Third World peoples. They also seemed to believe that once they had proven their Marxist-Leninist credentials they could expect massive fraternal assistance from the Soviet Union and its allies. Ideology also engendered Grenada's insatiable appetite for military aid, which only the communist countries were prepared to supply in such quantities.

On the other hand, the need for aid from all possible sources did temper the NJM's public ideological thrust. The NJM regime could not afford to alienate potential sources of aid by declaring openly its communist allegiance. This consideration, as well as the fear of provoking a violent reaction at home or from the United States, explains the paradox of PRG foreign policy: its obvious pro-Soviet stance, but rhetorical non-alignment; its constant, vehement condemnation of "imperialism," a word which it used strictly in the Soviet sense as a synonym for U.S. foreign policy—along with repeated claims of wanting "good relations" with the United States. The PRG sought to portray itself to the world as a plucky David struggling for independence against the

North American Goliath; a poor but proud developing country trying manfully to better its lot, but being bullied and pressured at every turn by "imperialism." Nor was this merely a sham: the NJM leaders themselves believed it implicitly.

The foremost friend and sponsor of the NJM regime was always Cuba. It is a misapprehension to believe that Cuba *controlled* the PRG, or tried to. The Grenada documents do not support this thesis. On the other hand, Cuba's influence was profound. Cuba was the only established communist state in a position to give the NJM real moral and material support in its early days, and Bishop and his colleagues made no secret of their admiration for Castro and his revolution.

In his address marking the first anniversary of the NJM coup, Bishop acknowledged that "if there had been no Cuban revolution in 1959 there could have been no Grenadian revolution in 1979." Not only had Cuba supported the coup itself, but by the end of the NJM's first full month in power, Castro had supplied the new regime with 3,800 infantry weapons and 36 artillery pieces, as well as advisors to teach the PRA how to use them. Cuba also provided civilian advisors for a wide range of party and government activities, including health, infrastructure development, the fisheries project, education, and propaganda. According to a report from Grenada's embassy in Havana, there were by 1980 "22 different areas of collaboration with Cuba plus seven areas requiring constant consultation." In return, Grenada was an unfailingly loyal ally. No doubt Bishop meant what he said in a private letter to Castro: "In whatever ways and at whatever price the heroic internationalist people of Cuba can always count on [the] total solidarity, support and cooperation of the Grenada revolution."[42]

The Cubans, for their part, saw in Grenada an opportunity to enhance their prestige as a leader of Third World revolution and increase their influence in the Carribean. The latter consideration was especially important after the bitterly disappointing electoral defeat of Michael Manley's pro-Cuban government in Jamaica in 1980. Jamaica's new Prime Minister, Edward Seaga, had cut off diplomatic relations with Havana because of "unacceptable involvement by Cuba in our domestic affairs."[43]

Grenada's international airport was the centerpiece of this symbiotic relationship. The PRG hoped the airport would become the cornerstone of a new tourist industry that would provide a quick and steady flow of foreign exchange and help finance the rest of the government's economic program. Over the years, as other development projects languished and failed, the significance of the airport grew even greater. It became a token of the PRG's determination to achieve its economic goals against all odds. To the Cubans, it was a highly visible symbol of their ability to provide fraternal aid: Cubans and Grenadians working side by side to put Grenada on the map. The airport would prove that socialist countries took care of their own. At the same time, it would extend the reach of Cuban jetfighters throughout the region, and provide an important refueling station for Cuban transport aircraft on their way to resupply Cuban forces in Angola.[44]

The NJM regime was helpful in Havana's efforts to cultivate contacts with the small island states. Representatives from Cuba were invited to "party-building seminars" and youth-group meetings hosted by Grenada for the various leftist organizations of the region, and Grenada provided briefings and documents to the Cubans on political conditions in the Eastern Caribbean. In 1980, Richard Jacobs, then Ambassador to Havana, sought to use his good offices with the Bahamas government to smooth over relations with Cuba after a Cuban MIG sank a Bahamian vessel in Bahamian waters. "I have arranged for the leaders of the Vanguard party—a small socialist party there—to visit Cuba, as well as a trade union delegation," Jacobs wrote. "This will be helpful to Cuba in making some contacts there."

Cuba cultivated a close relationship with Richard Hart, a veteran Jamaican communist acting as Grenada's attorney general. A 1982 letter to Hart from the Centro de Estudios Sobre America in Havana, one of a number exchanged between Hart and the Cubans, thanked him for "papers and things" which he had sent and which "have been of vital importance for our work in the Caribbean." It went on to solicit his help for Cuban efforts to establish contacts with the Organization of Eastern Caribbean States (OECS).[45]

If Grenada was Cuba's entree to the eastern Caribbean, Cuba was Grenada's pipeline to the Soviet bloc. Diplomatic relations between the PRG and the Soviet Union were established through Cuban channels in a communique signed in Havana on December 7, 1979. In May–June 1980, Bernard Coard followed up with a trip to the Soviet Union and Eastern Europe and signed a party-to-party accord with the Soviets, as well as some minor aid and trade agreements. But even after that trip, much of the regular diplomatic business between Grenada and the Soviet Union was carried on in Havana. Two of the three Soviet-Grenadian military assistance treaties were signed there, the first on October 27, 1980. Even as late as 1983, after a Grenadian embassy was established in Moscow, Ambassador Richard Jacobs reported back to St. George's that one principal reason the Soviets had decided to support the PRG was that "Cuba has strongly championed our cause."[46]

The Soviets, in fact, were slow and cautious in establishing links with the PRG. Ambassador Jacobs attributed this to their having been burned "quite often in the past by giving support to governments which have either squandered that support, or turned around and become agents of imperialism, or lost their power. One is reminded of Egypt, Somolia, Ghana, and Peru." In meetings in 1981 and 1982 the Soviets accepted that the NJM was a communist party, but questioned Grenada's membership in the Socialist International which, they cautioned, "has its own aims." Grenada's representatives "had to point out that the NJM's membership in the SI is a tactic." The Grenadians' impression was that the Soviets were still sizing up the NJM.[47]

Another impediment to closer economic relations was Grenada's spotty record in using the aid it received and in living up to trade agreements. Ambassador Jacobs complained to St. George's, for example, that out of 80 university or technical scholarships offered by the Soviets from 1981 to 1983, Grenada had used only 18. This created a bad impression. Because of bad communications on Grenada's part, Soviet tractors had arrived in Grenada without hoses, and military vehicles without needed spare parts. A Hungarian study of Grenada's request for agricultural assistance concluded that "Grenada is not yet sufficiently developed to" make use of "any kind of professional aid." Bulgaria complained that it had not received a shipment of nutmegs promised in exchange for an ice-making plant. East German authorities were horrified at the suggestion that Grenada might want to renegotiate an agreement on deliveries of bananas.[48]

Finally, the Soviets did not wish to be embroiled in a confrontation with the United States over a small and distant island. Soviet trade officials warned, for example, that while they were trying to give Grenada "every support possible," their assistance "must never be provocative from the point of view of the international situation." In a meeting with Bishop in April 1983, Gromyko himself hinted of the same concern, remarking in an avuncular tone that the leftist parties and groups in the Caribbean must "exercise great care and flexibility so as not to provoke the imperialist forces to smash the progressive forces." He commended Bishop for the "low-key way in which the NJM had been conducting seminars for radical Caribbean parties."[49]

Nevertheless, relations with the USSR had intensified noticeably by 1983, and aid and trade from the Soviet bloc were increasing. The NJM signed party-to-party accords with several Eastern European countries. The PRG reached trade agreements with Bulgaria, Czechoslovakia, and East Germany as well as the USSR. The East Germans were particularly helpful, providing military trucks, equipment for security forces, a printing machine, and technicians to upgrade Grenada's dilapidated telephone system. East Berlin was also eager to explore the idea of establishing its own relay station in Grenada for broadcasting in English to the Americas, an agreement which, it pointed out, "would guarantee the presence of GDR technicians in Grenada."[50]

From the Soviets, Grenada received some construction materials for a new NJM party headquarters, some cars and buses, a few small generators, a light airplane, and a number of scholarships for academic, technical, ideological, military, and security training. There were also some trade agreements to purchase supplies of Grenadian spices and cocoa. Toward the end, the USSR was sending science teachers to Grenada and developing a larger diplomatic presence there, probably a portent of closer ties to come.

As indicated by the captured documents and arms caches, Soviet military and security assistance started slowly but became quite generous. The first "top secret" arms agreement between the USSR and Grenada, signed in Havana on October 27, 1980 provided for 4.4 million rubles worth of "special and other equipment" to be provided by the Soviets through 1980–81. The "special equipment" specified included 12 mortars, 24 anti-tank grenade launchers, 54 machine guns, 1000 submachine guns, 18 anti-aircraft mounts and other weapons, communications and support equipment, ammunition and spare parts. It also provided for training Grenadian servicemen, in the USSR to use the new equipment.[51]

A second military aid agreement, signed in Havana on February 9, 1981, provided for 5 million rubles worth of equipment to be delivered through 1983. This agreement included eight armored personnel carriers and uniforms for an army of 6,000, as well as more arms, ammunition, etc.[52] A third secret agreement, signed this time in Moscow on July 27, 1982, raised the stakes significantly. By 1985 the Soviets were to deliver equipment to support a much more serious military effort: 50 armored personnel carriers, 60 mortars, 60 anti-tank and other heavy guns, 50 portable rocket launchers, 50 light anti-tank grenade launchers, 2,000 submachine guns and much more. The 1982 agreement also provided for equipment for Grenada's internal security forces — weapons intended for use on the Grenadian people: infrared viewers, videotape recorders, tape recorders, cameras, television equipment and other equipment designed for clandestine intelligence gathering.[53]

Despite this steadily increasing military and security assistance, on balance the PRG was disappointed with the level of Soviet support, which lagged far behind Grenada's escalating economic needs. Soviet officials drove hard bargains on trade agreements, pointing out that the USSR had no interest in purchasing 1,000 tons of nutmeg, as requested by Grenada, since it only consumed 200–300 tons per year, and that Ministry of Trade policy required any such purchases to be made "at the world market price or below." Ambassador Jacobs in Moscow anticipated a cool reception there for the PRG's 1983 proposal for establishing a "bank

of last resort" in COMICON for "countries of socialist orientation," as an alternative to the IMF. And when Bishop appealed
directly to Gromyko in their April 1983 meeting for a $6 million
grant or loan, the Soviets temporized until July and then refused,
saying they understood this money was to come from France.[54]

Over time, the PRG concluded that if Grenada was to be
accorded a higher rank in Moscow's order of priorities—as
Nicaragua, for example, clearly was—it would have to prove
that it could play a useful role for the Soviets on the world stage.
It had tried to do so from the beginning in the United Nations,
where it unfailingly voted with the Soviets, and defended the
Soviet position on every issue. For example, Cuba and Grenada
were the only countries in the Western Hemisphere to oppose a
1980 U.N. resolution calling on the Soviets to withdraw from
Afghanistan. "Considering the risks that we have taken on this
and other matters," Jacobs wrote from Moscow, the Soviets had
"every reason to be satisfied" with Grenada's performance in
support of them.[55] But obviously more was needed:

> For Grenada to assume a position of increasingly greater impor-
> tance [in the Soviets' eyes], we have to be seen influencing at least
> regional events. We have to establish ourselves as the authority on
> events in at least the English-speaking Caribbean, and be the spon-
> sor of revolutionary activity and progressive developments in this
> region at least.[56]

* * *

The PRG's relations with its Caribbean neighbors, as well as
with the United States to some extent, were reminiscent of
Moscow's two-tiered relations with the West after 1917. At one
level, through its Ministry of Foreign Affairs, Grenada maintained
more or less conventional diplomatic contacts with other governments in the region. At another level, Grenada acted consciously
as an agent of world revolution in the region. The NJM's International Relations Committee supported the activities of leftist
movements throughout the Caribbean and offered Grenada as a
training ground and safe haven for those movements. In return,

those movements provided propaganda and political support for the PRG, information (and sometimes sensitive intelligence) on political affairs in their countries, and personnel to staff the PRG itself.

This last benefit was particularly important to the NJM in view of the dearth of politically reliable Grenadians to fill government posts. In fact, to some degree the People's Revolutionary Government of Grenada was a collaborative effort of the radical intelligentsia from throughout the Caribbean.

Jamaica gives a good example. The PRG had cordial dealings with the democratic socialist government of Michael Manley. But it had much closer ties to the Workers' Party of Jamaica (WPJ) led by Trevor Munroe. The WPJ was an avowedly communist organization that Richard Jacobs described to the Soviets as "the only authentic serious Marxist-Leninist group in Jamaica."[57] As early as October 1979, Munroe dispatched a team of trusted WPJ members to Grenada to work with the NJM and receive security training. By 1981, the Jamaican contingent was functioning as a formal branch of the WPJ within Grenada, seconded to the NJM Political Bureau with "the right to take the initiative in making suggestions to" the NJM on the revolutionary process.[58]

Munroe made a number of suggestions and proposals, expecting and receiving a certain deference from NJM leaders as a senior communist in the region. He advised Bishop by letter on how to handle the unions in the wake of the 1981 public workers' strike, and coordinated closely on plans for promoting the other radical parties in the Caribbean. Munroe even drafted his Jamaican colleagues to serve in responsible posts for the PRG—Denzil Wilks to head the Marketing and National Imports Board, Charles Campbell to serve in the Ministry of Education, and Brian Meeks to teach socialism classes for the Ministry of National Mobilization, to name a few. He recruited elsewhere around the Caribbean as well. In January 1981, for example, he reported back to Bishop on conversations with Patrick Emmanuel in Barbados, whom he recommended as a possible choice for a high foreign affairs post despite his "petty-bourgeois egoism and ideological reservations on Marxism-Leninism." An NJM Political Bureau meeting in 1982 noted that "our mass media will collapse if the WPJ comrades were to leave." In return, Munroe requested Bishop's and Coard's help in persuading Cuba to restore the "special programme with us" in Jamaica, which had been suspended since Seaga's victory. And he asked the NJM to accept one or two people in the meantime "for special training by your specialists in expls [explosives?]."

Among its non-socialist neighbors, the NJM cultivated close ties with leftists in Trinidad, particularly Michael Als of the People's Progressive Movement and Allan Alexander, an important source of legal advice to the PRG. Ralph Gonsalves of the St. Vincent United People's Movement was, Richard Jacobs told the Soviets, "a clear, consistent and reliable Marxist-Leninist" who "can be helped at all levels without fear of compromise." The NJM also worked closely with Tim Hector of the Antigua Caribbean Liberation Movement (ACLM). A top-secret report of Grenada's security service recounted Hector's assistance in procuring sensitive Antigua government documents, and recommended that two ACLM comrades be brought to Grenada for security training.[59]

The PRG's formal diplomatic relations with the governments it was working to undermine were understandably cool. The PRG was barely on speaking terms with the governments of Jamaica (under Seaga) and Trinidad, although the NJM leaders worked and schemed assiduously to normalize relations with Port-of-Spain. Most of Grenada's relations with Caribbean states were through meetings of regional institutions such as CARICOM and the OECS, at which Grenada made a point to be present to protect its interests. On no account did the PRG want to alienate its neighbors so deeply that they would be tempted later to collaborate openly with "imperialism" against it.

The one country in the Western Hemisphere toward which the NJM regime cultivated a truly "fraternal" relationship, other than Cuba, was Nicaragua. The PRG prided itself on having been the second country to recognize Ortega's government in 1979. The two governments supported each other faithfully in international fora, and even exchanged token foreign aid. The NJM also organized rallies for El Salvador, briefed the FMLN/FDR guerrillas there on the Caribbean political situation, and advised them on ways to participate in the 1983 CARICOM summit meeting. But the Grenadians drew the line at overt military assistance. Grenada's own sources of supply forbade it. And besides, "the main right-wing propaganda thrust for the CARICOM summit is that we are training foreigners to export revolution. Hence the need to be careful about this."[60]

The PRG's relations with the rest of the Third World were determined mainly by the prospects of aid. Bishop courted the Arab states devotedly. In exchange for some anti-Zionist statements that fit in comfortably with NJM ideology, he returned from a 1980 tour of the Middle East with about $10 million in grants. Technical assistance agreements were signed with Libya, Algeria, Syria, and Iraq, and Algeria pledged to supply all the oil and gas used by machines on Grenada's international airport project. In fact, Arab aid to the airport project was so extensive that in October 1982 the Islamic Foundation wrote to St. George's, requesting that the main access road to the airport be named Palestine Drive.

Grenada's membership in the democratic Socialist International was also partly connected with aid prospects. The SI had mobilized economic support for Nicaragua, and might be persuaded to do the same for Grenada. The PRG's main interest in the SI, however, was to use it as an instrument against the U.S. and U.S. policy in the Caribbean and Central America, and to mobilize sympathy and support for the NJM regime in particular. As Marxist-Leninists, the NJM leaders had misgivings about joining a social-democratic organization. But they decided it would be tactically expedient to do so.

From the time it formally joined the Socialist International in November 1980, the PRG sought to manipulate the organization into an overtly anti-American posture. For instance, at a March 1981 emergency SI meeting, Grenada opposed adding the names of Cuba and the Soviet Union to a resolution demanding that outside powers cease sending arms into El Salvador. According to Unison Whiteman, "Grenada pointed out that ... SI should not speculate on where the freedom fighters are getting arms from; that, in any event, we should not equate arms for the oppressors with weapons to defend the people in their just struggle."

Whiteman was satisfied with a compromise wording that "name[d] no country" but made it clear that the U.S. was being condemned. And he was exultant that U.S. Ambassador-at-Large Vernon Walters was refused the opportunity to submit proof of Cuban and Soviet arms supplies.[61]

The United States was the real focal point of PRG foreign policy. The basic foreign policy premise that the NJM brought with it when it came to power, a virtual article of faith that it seems never to have questioned, was that its own policy was by definition non-aligned and peaceful, but that U.S. imperialism made good relations between the two governments nearly impossible. From the beginning of their rule, Grenada's new leaders anticipated enmity from the United States, and they continued to view every U.S. gesture in the light of this expectation. Negative reports on the Grenadian revolution in the American press were seen as evidence of Washington's anti-PRG propaganda and destabilization efforts, while positive media coverage was interpreted as an indication of Grenada's own success in "beating back imperialist lines" among the masses. On one occasion in early 1982, the Central Committee, noticing that the U.S. administration had not been criticizing the PRG lately, wondered whether this meant that the U.S. had decided to finish off El Salvador and Nicaragua first before attacking Grenada. The leaders came to the almost comic conclusion that "our ability to 'fight back' has shocked them," and that they "could therefore move to the stage of assassination attempts."[62]

Given the PRG policies regarding elections, human rights, and so forth, relations between Washington and St. George's were bound to be complicated. But the NJM's predisposition to suspect a sinister CIA plot behind every untoward event, domestic or foreign, whether objectively related to the U.S. or not, doomed any hope of establishing even a reasonably civil dialogue. Stung by Bishop's rhetoric, the U.S. began trying to set the record straight in private meetings and public statements, but finally resigned itself to ignoring most of what emanated from St. George's.

The PRG's first accusation against the United States was that it had given refuge to Eric Gairy and allowed him to plot a countercoup from American soil. On June 9, 1979, following Bishop's first public charges on the subject, the U.S. Embassy in Bridgetown received a note from the PRG, formally requesting Gairy's return. Kenrick Radix took up the subject in a visit to the State Department the following month, as did Sally Shelton, the new U.S. Ambassador, in her first call on Bishop on July 23. But only in August and September did the State Department first receive packets of documents purporting to be concrete evidence of Gairy's wrongdoing. In January 1980, after discussions between Bishop and U.S. officials, the U.S. agreed to send a Department of Justice extradition expert to Grenada to confer on the case.[63]

When the Department of Justice official arrived in St. George's in February, he was met by the legal advisor in the Ministry of Foreign Affairs, Ashley Taylor. After describing U.S. laws regarding extradition, the official pointed out three problems with the PRG's application: (1) the crimes with which Gairy was charged dated from five years back and thus fell outside of the U.S. statute of limitations; (2) the PRG had submitted only hearsay evidence; and (3) the offenses cited by the PRG were liable to be dismissed by a U.S. court as political offenses, for which extradition was impossible. Taylor asked whether extradition would be possible on other charges. The Department of Justice official advised him that financial crimes were more likely to produce results, and that Department of Justice lawyers could be made available to foreign governments to help with the complexities of preparing such a case. That afternoon the official paid a brief courtesy call on Attorney General Radix, who had meanwhile been briefed by Taylor. Radix indicated that he understood the situation, and said "you can now leave it to us."[64]

Embassy Bridgetown accordingly advised Washington to expect a request for legal assistance to prepare a new extradition request. Instead the PRG went to the media. In separate interviews in March 1980, Unison Whiteman and Bernard Coard claimed that the PRG had fulfilled all requirements for Gairy's extradition. Whiteman added that the U.S. authorities "appear to be dragging their feet." The U.S. responded with a public statement summarizing the gist of the Department of Justice's advice to Taylor, including the offer of legal assistance, and repeated its willingness to consider a properly documented extradition request.

The PRG never brought up the subject again. Subsequent events suggest that the government may have been more interested in making propaganda points than in getting Gairy back. For one thing, in June 1980, Lloyd Noel resigned his position as Acting Attorney General, later citing as one of his reasons the sudden loss of interest in the Gairy extradition case. And a letter from Taylor to Bishop, written as early as 1979, suggests that the leadership was aware that getting Gairy back might have undesirable consequences.[65]

One of the regime's more regular activities was discovering counter-revolutionary plots and invasion threats, which it invariably linked to the U.S. The first of these allegations was prompted on May 7, 1979, when a mentally disturbed American medical student set fire to the house in which he lived (in the "Carifta Cottages" complex, an area of no military significance). Almost simultaneously, a suspicious fire broke out in a tourist office in downtown St. George's. There was no evidence linking the U.S. in any way to either fire, and Bishop later agreed privately with an American Embassy official that the medical student was probably not responsible for his actions. Nevertheless, on May 8, Bishop went on the radio to accuse the CIA of plotting a campaign of "arson and violence" against Grenada.[66]

The second alleged plot was uncovered in October–November 1979, and was discussed in Chapter Two above. But on June 19, 1980, there was a real terrorist incident: a bomb exploded in a crowded stadium at Queen's Park just outside St. George's. The intended victims were obviously Bishop and the NJM leaders, most of whom were at a podium just above the blast, but who were shielded by a concrete beam. Instead the bomb killed three young women and injured nearly a hundred other bystanders. At 8:30 that evening, Bishop went on the air with an angry tirade opening with the words "today imperialism struck," and going on to recite a long list of atrocities (the Bay of Pigs, Vietnam, the assassination of Allende, etc.) for which "imperialism" was to blame, implying that the Queen's Park bombing was the latest of these.[67]

On June 24, the U.S. Embassy in Bridgetown sent a note to

the PRG stating categorically that no agency of the U.S. government was in any way involved in the bombing, and the PRG later acknowledged the note with appreciation. Nevertheless, when a second bomb exploded in northeastern Grenada on June 25, the PRG blamed it directly on "imperialism and the CIA." On July 2, the PRG Mission to the United Nations circulated a formal diplomatic note to all missions, alleging that "imperialism and its local agents had attempted the murder of Prime Minister Maurice Bishop" and his entire cabinet. No proof was ever offered and the evidence indicates that the bombing incidents were the result of factional strife within the NJM.[68]

Beginning in August 1981, the NJM got a real scare. The U.S. and NATO forces staged one of an ongoing series of major maritime maneuvers in the Atlantic and the Caribbean, this one entitled "Ocean Venture 81." The scenario included the seizure of American hostages by an eastern Caribbean island state called "Amber," and a landing by U.S. troops on "Amber"—represented by Vieques Island off Puerto Rico—to rescue the hostages.

The NJM leaders were truly alarmed. They were sure "Amber" stood for Grenada. Their fears were heightened by a message from Castro indicating he had evidence that the U.S. had decided to overthrow the PRG that summer. The PRG launched a worldwide diplomatic initiative to solicit help in warding off an imminent invasion, which Bishop claimed would occur no later than November 1, 1981. The PRA and the militia were mobilized and sent off with much fanfare on "route marches" to the beach, to practice defending Grenada against the invading hordes.[69]

The invasion, of course, never materialized. But the NJM leaders may have been right about "Amber" representing Grenada. In November 1979, Kenrick Radix, never noted for his sense of discretion, had told a European delegate at the U.N. that he thought the taking of U.S. hostages in Iran was justified because the U.S. had taken in the Shah. He added that he would favor Grenada taking American hostages to pressure the United States into returning Gairy. Though at the time Washington was acutely sensitive to such threats, U.S. officials decided Radix was not serious, and let the matter drop. But shortly afterwards, PRG Labour Minister Selwyn Strachan reportedly made a remark echoing Radix's view. Moreover, the PRG had been detaining one American since July 9 without charges and without access to a consular officer, apparently in retaliation for the arrest of NJM gun-runners Jim Wardally and Chester Humphrey.[70] Given these facts, the state of U.S.-Grenada relations, and the hundreds of American students at the medical school, the PRG may have been right to interpret the "Amber" exercise as a warning. In any case, if it was a message, the PRG got it. They concluded that nothing was more likely to promote a U.S. military action against them than a threat to the Americans on the island. This perception may well have helped save American lives in the final chaotic days of the NJM.

There was another invasion scare in March 1983, in response to a speech by President Reagan referring to "Castroite control over the island of Grenada," and remarks by Defense Secretary Caspar Weinberger pointing to the threat of a "buildup of Soviet and Cuban military power" in Central America and the Caribbean. The PRG once again sounded the alarm, launching a renewed diplomatic offensive abroad and another military mobilization at home. By this time, though, both foreign and domestic audiences were growing jaded with the NJM's constant harping about "imperialist" plots, and there was little response.[71]

The PRG frequently charged the U.S. with "economic destabilization," including discouraging American tourists from visiting Grenada and excluding Grenada from aid and disaster relief programs. The first of these charges was untrue: the U.S. never issued a travel advisory against Grenada, although it was sorely tempted to do so. The second charge was partially true: the U.S. turned down the PRG's request for aid in the wake of Hurricane Allen in 1980. The U.S. agreed with the Windward Island Banana Association (WINBAN) that the aid should be concentrated on St. Vincent, St. Lucia, and Dominica, which had been hardest hit. The United States also excluded Grenada from receiving a share of U.S. funds offered to the Caribbean Development Bank for school construction and for social services. Washington did this partly as a signal of its displeasure over the PRG's neglect of elections and human rights, and partly because it viewed the PRG's investment program, focused as it was on the new international airport, as unsound. Similarly, the U.S. sought to block a 1981 IMF loan to Grenada, mainly on the grounds that the money would be used to replace funds siphoned off elsewhere to pay for the airport.[72]

The airport, which the U.S. came to view as a potential Soviet-Cuban military asset, was at the hub of U.S.-PRG friction. The idea of building an international airport at Point Salines went back at least 40 years. Point Salines would be a safer place to land than hilly Grenville, where Pearls Airport is located. There was room for a runway long enough for international jets, and it was closer than Grenville to St. George's and the main tourist resorts. But because of the enormous cost involved, and because the Grenadian tourist industry was too small to support an airport of that size, outside financing had been hard to find.[73]

Before taking power, the NJM had opposed the airport, partly because it viewed the tourist industry as a means of capitalist infiltration and exploitation. Ironically, the NJM also feared that, under Gairy, the airport would become a Pentagon asset. As Bishop argued, "The importance of this installation for our country is obvious . . . But its importance for the military circles in the Pentagon is also obvious, given Grenada's strategic position in the Caribbean and on the routes to Africa and Europe." But, within a couple of months after the coup, Bishop changed his mind and persuaded Canada to undertake a new feasibility study of the airport. Even before the study was done, Bishop announced that Cuba would take the lead in developing the project, providing equipment, materials, and 250 laborers. Grenada would have to raise about half the cost of the project itself, however, and this the PRG set out to do.

The U.S. not only refused to aid the project, it went to some lengths to persuade Western European nations to refuse as well. Washington was convinced the NJM cared more about the political and military benefits of the airport than about building the tourist industry. The Cuban involvement alarmed Washington initially, and subsequent developments did nothing to ease those fears. Only one airline had responded to PRG feelers on the use of the airport and that one, Eastern Airlines, had reportedly told the PRG that a minimum of 2,100 rooms would be required to justify regular service. Grenada had under 1,000 rooms, and there was no evidence of a major effort to build more. In an interview with *Newsweek* magazine in early 1980, Bishop had refused to rule out Cuban or Soviet military use of the airport: "Suppose there's a war next door in Trinidad, where the forces of fascism are about to take control, and the Trinidadians need external assistance. Why should we oppose anybody passing through Grenada to assist them?" At a conference of the Worker's Party of Jamaica in December 1981 the NJM's Selwyn Strachan stated that the Point Salines airport would be available for use by Cuba and the Soviet Union. Also, a diary belonging to Central Committee member Liam James, recovered after the October 1983 intervention, contained the notation from a March 1980 meeting: "Airport will be used for Cubans and Soviets Military." (According to a CBS poll taken one week after the October '83 intervention, 65 percent of the Grenadian people agreed the airport "was going to be used mostly for Cuban and Soviet military purposes.")[74]

In the end, little Western European aid was forthcoming. The project went ahead nonetheless, and became an enormous drain on the Grenadian economy. From the Cuban perspective, on the other hand, it was a first-rate investment: it provided jobs for hundreds of underemployed Cuban workers, many of them unskilled; it was a highly visible showpiece of Cuban aid for a fraternal state; and it gave Cuba enormous leverage over Grenada economically, politically, and militarily. When completed, the airport would have been at least as great an asset to Cuba as to Grenada.[75]

U.S. "sabotage" of Western European funding for the airport became a featured item in the long list of PRG grievances against the United States. The clash between U.S. and PRG interests in this instance was obvious enough. But Washington was puzzled by the numerous other PRG charges of U.S. "destabilization" that were manifestly absurd, and that inevitably made it impossible to establish the "good relations" the PRG repeatedly claimed it wanted with the United States. Reporting on an internal crackdown in Grenada coincident with the 1981 invasion scare, Embassy Bridgetown expressed its belief that "the PRG makes its charges with indeterminate proportions of genuine alarm and calculated cynicism. Obviously, the bogey of CIA mercenaries serves PRG propaganda interests, but observers of the PRG feel also that Bishop and his colleagues are really afraid of 'destabilization.' It is clear from their works and actions that they subscribe fully to the school of thought which sees and exposes CIA agents at every turn, guided by . . . the work of Philip Agee and other like him."[76] (Agee, the ex-CIA agent who makes his living exposing his former colleagues, was granted a Grenadian passport after his U.S. passport was revoked.)

In both the government and the press there was some speculation that Bishop's last trip to the United States, in June 1983, was part of an effort to improve relations. Bishop's public statements on that trip, for example, were unusually conciliatory in tone. But internal party documents suggest the primary purpose of the trip was to put pressure on the Reagan administration by cultivating support for the NJM among sympathetic groups in the public and in Congress. It was, in short, a public relations and lobbying campaign. A Political Bureau meeting identified three "strategic objectives" for the visit: conveying an image to the American press and public of Bishop as a "sober and reliable statesman"; developing "unshakeable links" with the U.S. black community; and promoting tourism, mainly among blacks.

The American press later put great emphasis on the one substantive event of Bishop's trip, his meeting with National Security Adviser William Clark. After Bishop's murder, some media outlets claimed that the meeting had been a missed opportunity, that Bishop had harbored great hopes for better relations, and that Clark, or the President, had lost a chance to embrace Bishop and lure him peacefully out of the Soviet-Cuban orbit. This is an unlikely interpretation. U.S. government spokesmen confirm that Bishop did ask for improved relations, but there was little new about such a request. What would have been new was a change in Bishop's rhetoric or behavior towards the U.S. He had only four months to live, months full of turmoil. There was little chance to test his sincerity. However, a memorandum from Richard Jacobs, PRG Ambassador to Moscow, suggests Bishop may have been sincere: Jacobs, acting on instructions, refused to brief the Russians on the details of Bishop's meeting with Clark. Nevertheless, the Political Bureau's top-secret analysis of the trip did not stress Bishop's meeting with Clark, but dwelt at length on the Prime Minister's success in impressing Congressmen and the media:

> It was clear that all these editorial personnel had one major objective; to assess . . . whether we are communists or more "Revolutionary Nationalists." And this is where the proof of our success in those meetings lie [sic], for it is obvious that almost all of them went away, maybe seeing us a bit naive, in a specific context, but . . . brave little fellows who are much more nationalists than communists . . . [77]

THE POLITICAL PROGRAM

In the autumn of 1982, the NJM Central Committee distributed to party members a key policy statement over which it had labored and debated for months: Maurice Bishop's "Line of March for the Party" speech. Though delivered by Bishop at a major party assembly, it was largely a collective effort in which the party leaders assessed their revolution. Obviously it was not yet a socialist revolution: the economy, and above all the working class itself, were still too underdeveloped. Even the leaders of the revolution were not of working class origin but represented, as they themselves admitted, the radicalized youth of the petty bourgeoisie. The leaders' aim, therefore, was to lead the revolution from its current stage of "socialist orientation" to the higher stage of "socialist *construction*." To do this they would have to overcome bourgeois influences in themselves and the society as a whole. Only when this was accomplished and the working class became truly the dominant revolutionary force, would the revolution acquire the "political essence" that would make socialism attainable.[78]

There was something mystical-sounding not only in this discussion of "political essence," but in other examples of the NJM's forays into the realm of Marxist theory as well. The party, presumably, and Bishop almost certainly, had originally adopted

Marxist-Leninist ideology as a means to an end, for Marxism-Leninism purported to be an exact science whose rules, properly applied, would inevitably lead to the development of a just and prosperous society. But having accepted on faith the premise that "correct" Marxist theory and practice would produce the desired results, the NJM leaders made ideology an end in itself and the measure by which every initiative was measured. The purpose of the revolution came to be the realization of a Marxist-Leninist model at all costs. "Scientific socialism" became a dogma whose tenets were beyond question among the elect; an arcane wisdom that set party members apart from the "masses" and could be invoked as a sufficient guide and justification for all the NJM's radical policies. This promise of a "secret knowledge" was fatally appealing to the hubris and impatience of a young intellectual elite.

Since the party was a "vanguard," it had to be selective, or so argued chief theoretician Bernard Coard. Under Coard's influence, criteria for party membership were progressively tightened. By 1982 one had to pass through three distinct stages of apprenticeship— Potential Applicant, Applicant, and Candidate Member—on the way to becoming a full member, and the party was considering adding a fourth category of "Prospective Potential Applicant." The aim of all this was not only to discourage spies, but to guard against the ever-present danger of petty-bourgeois influences creeping into the party to weaken its political consciousness and dedication.[79]

The term "petty bourgeois" did not refer only to a particular class. It also described certain character traits unworthy of a dedicated revolutionary: laziness, personal ambition, lack of objectivity, and above all, lack of "discipline." A class-conscious revolutionary was firm and disciplined, and so forth, and was expected to act "ruthlessly" in purging petty-bourgeois influences from himself, the party, and society at large. As party members and applicants were told: "Being a Communist, comrades, means becoming a different kind of person."

Such words—"firm," "disciplined," "ruthless"—peppered the internal communications of the NJM, particularly those issuing from the desks of Coard and his closest associates. A document designed to help put the party "on a *firmer* Leninist footing" recommends, for example, taking a "*firmer* line on the question of study" and "a *firm* position . . . on the question of priorities, so that the need to *ruthlessly* stick to priorities could be built into party comrades"; and developing "a system for *mannersing* [disciplining] any comrade from top to bottom who fails to fulfill his task" [emphasis added]. The NJM was obsessed with discipline, reflecting perhaps the zeal of its European and North American-trained leaders to impose on their society the values of the Colonial powers, which they themselves had had to absorb.[80]

The job of the elite was to lead the masses forward along the line of march established by the party. This meant staying close to the people to understand their mood, their immediate concerns, and the state of their consciousness, but *not* being absorbed into them. Rather, the dedicated revolutionary would use his intimacy with the masses and their confidence in him to lead them forward step by step from their current ideological backwardness to a higher understanding of their objective class interests. According to an NJM instructional pamphlet:

> The duty of the vanguard . . . is to work patiently every day to prove to other workers, from their own experience, that there is no future except through greater unity, greater organization, greater struggle. Ultimately more and more workers will see the light, overcome the obstacles of capitalism and follow the leadership of the vanguard.[81]

In the task of enlightening the workers there were three main tools: propaganda, theoretical instruction, and practical instruction in the class struggle, including political activism.

Mass media was one of the most important instruments of propaganda. Both Lenin's writings and the NJM's own experience had led it to devote much effort and expense to putting out the *New Jewel* newspaper in its opposition years. The party also used public meetings, "block raps" for youth, house-to-house visits, and graffiti to publicize its view. Upon taking power it immediately converted Radio Grenada to propaganda purposes, renaming it Radio Free Grenada, and eventually supplemented it with Television Free Grenada. It expanded its newspaper activities. In imitation of other communist regimes it launched a print organ for every segment of society: *Worker's Voice* for the workers, *Cutlass* for the agro-proletariat, *Fight* for the youth, and several others. (These efforts were not very successful, and only the *New Jewel* and the established *Free West Indian* published regularly). All these activities, as well as the Government Information Service responsible for external propaganda, were coordinated under the State Propaganda Committee, which in turn reported to Coard's Organizing Committee.[82]

Theoretical instruction was carried on both within the NJM for party members and in the society at large through a variety of institutions. It consisted mainly of studies of Marxist-Leninist classics, particularly the works of Lenin himself. These were supplemented by approved Soviet treatises on the nature of Third World revolutions (the USSR being accepted as the final authority on Marxist theory), and by simplified instructional materials for teaching the basics of class struggle and anti-imperialism to initiates. More-sophisticated pupils within the party undertook topics such as "matter and forms of existence," "consciousness," and "fundamental laws of dialectics"; while army recruits or semi-literate peasants received instruction on "What is a Monopoly," "Imperialism — System of Violence, Murder and Wars," "Benefits of the Revolution," "Patriotism and Internationalism," and so on.[83]

Serious ideological study was mandatory for party members at all levels, but party leaders felt that this instruction had to be extended to the whole society. For this purpose, the NJM began instituting special socialism classes. Urban workers were the first priority, with special "crash" courses being offered to shop stewards, trade union leaders, and other influential people who could in turn tutor others. As the people grew disenchanted with the revolution, the party reacted by extending the socialism classes to a broader audience and demanding attendance. In August 1983, Minister of National Mobilization Selwyn Strachan circulated a stern memo to all government ministries and state enterprises, declaring that "Worker Education Classes" were regarded as essential to raising the efficiency, productivity, and political consciousness of workers; that for these reasons the classes were held during working hours and attendance was compulsory. "Absentism [sic] without an acceptable excuse will be viewed as absence from work." At about the same time Strachan also approached C. F. Toppin, a leader of the business community, to advise him of PRG intentions to start classes throughout the private sector. Originally the socialism classes were meant as a tool for identifying loyal and active supporters of the revolution and recruiting them for the party. But as time went on they became equally important as a means of monitoring growing discontent and identifying "counter-revolutionaries."[84]

Practical experience in the class struggle came largely through the mass organizations, though these were also used for theoretical instruction. The mass organizations—the Parish Coordinating Bodies, trade unions, youth and women's organizations, and the militia—were the basic institutions of the NJM's concept of grassroots democracy. Their purpose was to involve everyone in the struggle, and thereby raise the level of class consciousness and ideological commitment. They were "to organize every worker, every farmer, every youth, every student, to organize all the people on behalf of the Revolution." A set of guidelines drafted by "Headache" Layne of the Central Committee to promote this goal explained that only a high level of activity would keep the people together. "The Revolution has to keep the people constantly mobilized [;] in this respect the mass activities of the revolution must be continued and stepped up."[85]

The Parish Coordinating Bodies were at the center of the mobilization process. They were composed of representatives of all the mass organizations in a particular parish, under the direction of senior party members acting, in effect, as political commissars. The PCBs provided political direction to the village and zonal councils at which citizens convened to discuss local and national issues. They saw to it that the tickets to these meetings were issued to reliable people, and that questions or suggestions that the party wanted to pose from the "grassroots" were introduced from the floor. The PCBs also coordinated mass rallies and demonstrations at the parish level. They also tried to ensure that all the mass organizations were fully involved in the programs of the revolution such as adult education, housing repair, and the primary health care campaign.[86]

The National Youth Organization was founded as the youth arm of the party in June 1978 through the efforts of Coard's OREL circle. Like OREL, it was conceived as an elite training ground for future party cadre, but in 1980 the NJM opened it to mass membership. Eighty groups were founded that year, and by 1981 the NYO claimed 185 groups (including seven in Havana) and nearly 8,000 members. Its primary function was mobilizing and indoctrinating young people to support the NJM. It particularly concentrated on increasing party influence in education and the armed forces. Its pre-teen element, the Young Pioneers, was charged with "the revolutionary and patriotic formation of our youths within the age range 6–12 years." An NYO training leaflet described it as "an anti-imperialist organization" which "constantly explains to the youths and students (not only to its own membership) . . . how imperialism as a system of exploitation is responsible for high unemployment, how it prevents them from having the adequate facilities for sports and culture, how it is responsible for the poverty of our nation. . . ."[87]

The National Women's Organization followed a similar course of development. Formed by the NJM in 1977 as the Progressive Women's Organization, the NWO was reorganized under its new name and opened up to general membership in May 1980. It paid particular attention to implementing party policy in areas of health, housing, birth control, child care and primary education. Under the leadership of radical feminist Phyllis Coard, it also became a strong advocate of women's rights within the NJM and led a campaign against sexual exploitation, an endemic problem in Grenadian society. Its self-described "overall priority objectives," however, were "to greatly raise the political [and] academic consciousness of all members of the NWO."[88]

The military was by definition involved in the practical side of the class struggle: the defense of the state and of the revolution were its primary concerns. But for that reason, and because the troops were a captive audience, it was also the ideal environment for political indoctrination. "Commissars" conducted political classes for NCOs and soldiers for one hour daily and for the militia once a week. Topics included the economy, foreign policy, the threat of imperialism, class and class struggles, the difference between aggressive and defensive war, and so on. Troops were also exposed to political lectures, radio broadcasts, films, books, pamphlets, meetings and discussions. The objective was to educate "the soldiers in a spirit of revolutionary ideals, hatred for the imperialist and enemies of the revolution." Other goals were to foster "an internationalist outlook" (no doubt with the aid of the many Cuban advisors and other non-Grenadian officers in the militia) and to strengthen the links of the military with the broader society, including building "in the masses of youth and children a love for the homeland and the armed forces." The latter purpose was achieved through close links with the NYO and the development of a Cadet Corps in the secondary schools. Ideally, the regime hoped to enlist all able-bodied civilians in the militia, which it regarded as a mass organization "for all the people."[89]

Even as the NJM tightened political control toward the end of its regime, one event raised hopes for an eventual liberalization: the PRG finally announced the appointment of a constitutional commission. These hopes were misplaced, however, for the new constitution was intended to be no more than window dressing, or, at worst, a refinement of the NJM's control mechanism.

Before 1982, party leaders showed no real interest in constitutional reforms, referring to them only as a long and complex process that would have to be completed before elections could be held. In April 1980 Herbert Blaize and the GNP drafted a constitution for a presidential system similar to that of the U.S. and sent it to Bishop. To allow the NJM time to consolidate its regime, Blaize and the GNP offered to not contest the first presidential elections, but only to bid for seats in the legislature. The request went unanswered, despite a renewal of the GNP's offer in October the same year.[90] By 1982, though, the NJM was growing concerned about Grenada's deepening isolation from the rest of the Caribbean, and saw a constitution as a way of cleaning up its image with its neighbors. There were many misgivings: the "level of class consciousness of the masses" was "still very low"; the right-wing bourgeoisie might be encouraged by such a move; the exercise would divert the country from efforts to build socialism; and it would "not be a guarantee of non-isolation from the English-Speaking Caribbean."

Although the Central Committee decided to proceed, the personnel selected for the Commission indicated the direction its work was intended to take: virtually all were trusted members or supporters of the NJM. Patrick Emmanuel, a political scientist with close ties to the PRG, commented in a May 1983 article, "While no very precise guidelines as to future state structure are evident, there is little doubt that the traditional system of parliamentary institutions cannot be re-established."[91]

Constitutions aside, the facts indicate the NJM intended to consolidate its regime into an openly Marxist system on the Soviet model by the mid- to late 1980s. Some progress had already been made toward the traditional communist goal of converting the apparatus of the state into an instrument of the party. Aside from placing NJM loyalists and their allies from around the Caribbean in positions of power, the NJM had created the Ministry of National Mobilization in August 1981 as a self-styled "people's ministry." Publicly, Minister Selwyn Strachan explained that its purpose was "to put pressure on the bureaucracy, to make sure it works and really gets thing done." But according to an internal Central Committee report, "in reality it meant that the Party would be having easier access to the financial and other resources of the state." State control of the economy through an expanding state sector, central planning, increased restrictions on banking and private enterprise, and the removal of education from church to state control were all further steps in the consolidation of NJM power.[92]

The fifth anniversary celebration of the revolution planned for March 13, 1984, was looked to as a real turning point by the NJM, and by most other Grenadians as well. The planned dedication of the international airport on that date would have provided an important symbolic testimony to the regime's determination to survive and prevail. It also would have provided an important physical guarantee of the NJM's future, since it would have put Cuban transports within easy reach of St. George's in any emergency. The party's secret plans for announcing a National

Labor Service at the same time—a move it knew would be deeply unpopular—hinted at the added authority it expected to gain from the airport opening. A constitution and Soviet-style elections would have followed eventually—probably by about 1986, after the first five-year plan had been introduced, and the NJM had held its first congress as a mature Marxist-Leninist party.[93] History, however, had other things in store.

NOTES

1. "Health—A Brief Survey," summary of PRG public health goals drafted about late 1980 (GD unnumbered) p. 1; "Attempts at Health Planning Process by Ministry of Health," document prepared about late 1981 (GD unnumbered); "Country Report to Pan American Sanitary Bureau from Grenada," prepared 1982 (GD unnumbered), pp. 1–2; "Draft Policy Statement on Health of the People's Revolutionary Government," date uncertain (GD unnumbered).
2. "Towards a Strategy for Health Education in Community Health—Community Participation," report prepared by Assistant Health Education Officer, June 30, 1980 (GD unnumbered); Candia Alleyne, "A Primary Health Care Project for St. David's," draft proposal submitted August 19, 1981 (GD unnumbered); Sunshine, *Peaceful Rev*, pp. 86–87.
3. E. Walrond and R. Carpenter, "Report on the Existing Clinical and Health Care Facilities in Grenada, With Special Reference to Teaching," dated November 1979 (GD unnumbered) p. 9; conversations with Dr. E. P. Friday (surgeon at St. George's General Hospital), Alister Hughes, and others.
4. "Health—A Brief Survey," p. 2; "Country Report to Pan American Sanitary Bureau"; Grenada, Ministry of Health, "Implementation of Resolution: Status of Implementations of Resolutions at April, 1982," (GD unnumbered) p. 2.
5. "Health—A Brief Survey," p.2; Walrond and Carpenter, "Report on the Existing Clinical and Health Care Facilities," p. 9.
6. Walrond and Carpenter, "Report on the Existing Clinical and Health Care Facilities," pp. 9–10; conversations with Dr. E. P. Friday, Dr. Adolf Bierzynski, and others. William C. Adams, "Grenada Update," *Public Opinion*, February/March 1984.
7. Letter to "Political Bureau, NJM" from Phyllis Coard (GD 101194);

Letter to "Brother & Comrade Maurice Bishop" from Dr. Beverley-Mae Fitch-Pole, Ex-Casualty Registrar, General Hospital, dated June 28, 1982 (GD 104259); conversations with Dr. E. P. Friday and others.

8. Sunshine, *Peaceful Rev*, p. 88; Submission to Cabinet from the Minister of Health and Housing dated February 18, 1980 (GD unnumbered); untitled, undated report on housing (GD unnumbered); conversations with Lyden Ramdhanny, Sebastian Thomas, Teddy Victor, and others.

9. Sunshine, *Peaceful Rev*, p. 87; "Community School Day Programme," report prepared about 1981 (GD unnumbered), p. 20; conversation with Beverley Steele, Resident Tutor, UWI Extension, Grenada; untitled report on conditions in schools (GD 103745), p. 4.

10. Maurice Bishop, "Education in the New Grenada," in Marcus and Taber, *Maurice Bishop Speaks*, pp. 42–47.

11. "C.P.E. Evaluation Congress," report dated October 18, 1980 (GD 002800), p. 5; Sunshine, *Peaceful Rev*, p. 82.

12. "Minutes of the Political Bureau," dated June 22, 1983 (GD 100291), p. 4; "C.P.E. Evaluation Congress," pp. 5–7; conversations with Beverley Steele and others, including teachers in Grenadian schools.

13. Bishop, "Education in the New Grenada," p. 45; Sunshine, *Peaceful Rev*, p. 84.

14. "Community School Day Programme," report dating from about 1981 (GD unnumbered), pp. 8–22.

15. Conversations with Beverley Steele and others.

16. Conversations with Beverley Steele, Brother Leonard of Presentation College, Archdeacon Hoskins Huggins (head of the Anglican Church in Grenada with responsibility for supervision of Anglican schools), and others.

17. "Education, Sport, Culture: Review & Perspectives," report submitted to the July 1983 plenary meeting of the NJM Central Committee (GD 103745), p. 4; "Minutes of the Organizing Committee," dated May 9, 1983 (GD unnumbered), pp. 3–4; untitled report on conditions in schools (GD 103745), pp. 6–8; conversations with Brother Leonard, Beverley Steele, Bishop Charles, and others. The Central Committee is hereafter referred to as CC; the Organizing Committee as OC; the Political Bureau as PB; the Economic Bureau as EB; and the Workers' Committee as WC.

18. Bernard Coard, in an address at the First International Solidarity Conference with Grenada, November 24, 1981, quoted in Sunshine, *Peaceful Rev*, p. 75.

19. Sunshine, *Peaceful Rev*, p. 75; conversation with Lyden Ramdhanny.
20. Sunshine, *Peaceful Rev*, pp. 75, 79–81.
21. "Line of March," pp. 2–32.
22. Notes from CC ideological study group (hereafter cited as SG) (GD 103632), dated September 19, 1980, October 12, 1980, and May 3, 1981.
23. Notes from SG dated October 10, 1980, October 22, 1982, and November 25, 1982.
24. Notes from SG dated September 21, 1980, October 23, 1982 and November 25, 1982; notes from a General Meeting of the NJM, dated January 24, 1983 (GD unnumbered).
25. Anthony P. Maingot, "The 'Modern' and the 'Conservative' in Antillean Political Thought," typed manuscript dated May 27, 1983.
26. "Ideas Concerning Land Reform," undated document apparently drafted about mid-late 1981 (GD 002600); notes from SG, October 12, 1980; "People's Law No. 33 of 1981: Land Development and Utilization Law," in *Grenada: The People's Laws* (St. George's: Government Printing Office, 1982), p. 147.
27. Notes from SG dated October 22 and 23, 1982.
28. "Report on Committee for Land Reform," undated document apparently drafted in late 1981 or 1982 (GD unnumbered); "People's Law No. 48 of 1982: A Law to amend the Land Development and Utilization Law 1981," in *Grenada: The People's Laws* (St. George's: Government Printing Office, 1982), p. 239; handwritten notes of a CC meeting dated March 1, 1982, taken down by Maurice Bishop on the back of "Ideas Concerning Land Reform"; handwritten notes of CC plenary dated July 15 and 16, 1983 (GD unnumbered).
29. "Progress Report of Commission No. 5," undated, signed by "A. John, Sgt., Chief of CMC" (GD 102602); "Brief Report on Land Reform Committee," undated (GD 002600).
30. "A General Guide on the Emulation Question," undated document (GD unnumbered).
31. "Statement from the Unions (G.U.T., T.A.W.U., P.W.U.) re: Salaries Negotiations with Government of Grenada," undated document from about February 1981 (GD 103488); "Big Salary Increases Now Mean Disaster for Grenada," undated typed propaganda sheet (GD unnumbered); conversation with Robert Robinson, former president of the PWU.
32. "Resolution of the Political Bureau," dated (by hand) March 4, 1981 (GD 104060); conversation with Robert Robinson.

33. Sunshine, *Peaceful Rev*, pp. 104–105; "Party Committee Reports and Workshop Reports Given to Members' Study, August 20–23rd, 1982" (GD 001939), pp. 10–11; conversation with Sebastian Thomas.
34. Conversation with Lyden Ramdhanny.
35. "Line of March," pp. 24–25.
36. "Summary of the Workings of the Central Committee from December 30th, 1981–February 12th, 1982" (GD 103745), pp. 4–7.
37. Minutes of CC meeting on the economy November 4–5, 1982 (GD 104060), pp. 3, 7; "Report on Grenada Agro Industries Ltd. (True Blue)," undated (GD 103470); "Emergency Plan for National Fisheries Company," dated (in Bishop's hand) October 1982 (GD 103470); confidential security report from Michael Roberts, Head of Special Branch, undated (first page missing) (GD 003071); notes from SG dated January 6, 1983; "National Co-operative Development Agency Report, 1st April–30th June, 1983" (GD 101198); conversations with Norbert Fletcher (former Permanent Secretary in PRG Ministry of Agriculture) and with members of the Tivoli farm cooperative.
38. Grenada, "Economic Memorandum," pp. 21–22; minutes of EB meeting, April 22, 1983 (GD 100297), pp. 6–7; conversation with Lyden Ramdhanny.
39. "Summary of . . . CC," p. 6; minutes of WC meeting, June 6, 1983 (GD unnumbered), p. 4; minutes of PB/EB meeting, August 31, 1983 (GD 104060), p. 7; conversations with Grenadian bankers and with Lyden Ramdhanny.
40. Grenada, Ministry of Finance and Planning, "Grenada—IMF Negotiations: Summary Report and Recommendations," dated August 30, 1983 (GD unnumbered); minutes of EB meeting, April 22, 1983, p. 6; minutes of CC plenary meeting, July 13–18, 1983, p. 34; minutes of meeting of the Committee of Economic Ministers, July 25, 1983 (GD 100554), p. 4; minutes of PB/EB meeting, August 3, 1983 (GD 104061), p. 4; minutes of PB/EB meeting, August 10, 1983 (GD 100282), pp. 6–7; minutes of PB/EB meeting, August 31, 1983, p. 6.
41. Minutes of PB/EB meeting, August 3, 1983, pp. 5–6; "Country's Finances Deeply in Red," *Grenadian Voice*, December 10, 1983, p. 1.
42. Maurice Bishop, "Forward Ever! Against Imperialism and Towards Genuine National Independence and People's Power," in Marcus and Taber, *Maurice Bishop Speaks*, p. 82; handwritten letter addressed to "Companero Fidel" and signed "Maurice Bishop,"

apparently dictated about early 1981 (GD unnumbered); U.S., Departments of State and Defense, *Grenada: A Preliminary Report* (Washington, 1983), p. 22; "General Report" from Embassy of Grenada in Havana, dated (by hand) September 17, 1980 (GD 000425), p. 5.

43. Letter to Maurice Bishop from Prime Minister Edward Seaga of Jamaica (GD 104265). The letter, ostensibly intended to explain Seaga's decision regarding Cuba, has the ring of an implicit warning to the NJM.

44. Cuba apparently used Barbados to some extent as a stopover for ferrying troops to Africa prior to 1975, but the practice was discontinued.

45. Grenada, NJM National Youth Organisation, "Document of the '2nd meeting of the Anti-Imperialist Youth and Students of the Caribbean'," dated September 1982 (GD 102521); "General Report" from Embassy Havana, p. 2; letter to Richard Hart from Isabel Jaramillo, Centro de Estudios Sobre America, dated November 21, 1982 (GD 105637).

46. "Agreements concluded between the Governments of the U.S.S.R. and Grenada," dated May 29, 1982 (GD 103902); "General Report" from Embassy Havana, p. 5; "Grenada's Relations with the USSR," report from Grenada's Ambassador to Moscow, Richard Jacobs, dated July 11, 1983 (GD unnumbered), p. 2; "Relations with the CPSU," undated report from Embassy of Grenada in the USSR (GD 103672), p. 1; U.S., "Grenada: A Preliminary Report," pp. 23–24.

47. "Report of Mission to Moscow 3rd to 10th December, 1981" (GD 103068), pp. 4–5; report to Maurice Bishop from Bernard Bourne in Embassy Moscow, dated June 30, 1982 (GD 104262), p. 2; "Grenada's Relations with the USSR," p. 2.

48. "Grenada's Relations with the USSR," pp. 3, 6; "Report by Dr. Sandor Hodossi, Scientific Deputy Assistant Manager, About the Mission to Grenada between April 22 and May 11, 1981," conveyed under cover of a memo from Grenada's ambassador to Venezuela, noting that Dr. Hodossi's report had been received from the Hungarian Embassy there (GD 105643), p. 20; Minutes of meeting of Committee of Economic Ministers, April 18, 1983 (GD 101166), p. 2.

49. "Report of Mission to Moscow," p. 4; "Record of Meeting between Prime Minister Maurice Bishop and First Deputy Prime Minister and Minister of Foreign Affairs Andrei Gromyko at the Kremlin April 15th, 1983," notes in unidentified handwriting (GD 104261), pp. 3–4.

50. "Agreement on Cooperation between the New JEWEL Movement of Grenada and the Socialist Unity Party of Germany for the Years 1982 to 1985," undated (GD 103896); "Meeting with GDR State Committee for Sound Broadcasting May 19th, 1983," memorandum dated May 25, 1983 and signed by W. Richard Jacobs (GD 102855); "Meeting with Prime Minister (Chairman of the Council of Ministers) of the GDR, 20/5/83, 1:30 p.m.," undated (GD 102855); "Draft Proposal of Protocol between the People's Revolutionary Government of Grenada and the Government of the Czechoslovak Socialist Republics on the Delivery of Goods," undated, prepared for signature sometime in September 1983 (GD 103858); "Agreement for Cooperation between the Bulgarian Communist Party and the New JEWEL Movement of Grenada for the period 1982–1983," undated (GD 103676); minutes of PB meeting, June 3, 1981 (GD 103448), p. 4; minutes of EB meeting, June 5, 1981 (GD unnumbered), p. 2; U.S., *Grenada: A Preliminary Report*, p. 24.

51. "Agreement between the Government of Grenada and the Government of the U.S.S.R. . . . ," Havana, Oct. 27, 1980, cited in *Problems of Communism* (United States Information Agency) July–August 1984, p. 11.

52. "Protocol to the Oct. 27, 1980, Grenada–U.S.S.R. agreement on arms deliveries," Havana, Feb. 9, 1981. Cited in *Problems of Communism*, July–August 1984, pp. 11–12.

53. "Agreement between the Government of Grenada and the Government of the U.S.S.R. . . . " Moscow, July 27, 1982. Cited in *Problems of Communism*, July–August 1984, p. 12.

54. Minutes of EB meeting, June 5, 1981, p. 2; "Report of Mission to Moscow," p. 11; "Grenada's Relations with the USSR," pp. 4, 8; telex from Ambassador Jacobs in Moscow to Prime Minister Bishop, dated July 18, 1983 (GD unnumbered). It is unclear whether a second appeal for the $6 million by way of an "urgent personal note" from Bishop to Andropov, recommended by Jacobs in a telex on July 21 (GD unnumbered), was ever sent or had any better effect.

55. "Grenada's Relations With the U.S.S.R.," p. 5.

56. *Ibid.*, pp. 5, 7.

57. "Report of Mission to Moscow," p. 16.

58. Letters to "Comrade Maurice Bishop" signed by Trevor Munroe, dated October 16, 1979 and March 11, 1981 (GD 104729, 104260).

59. "Report of Mission to Moscow," pp. 7–9; "Grenada's Relations

with the USSR," p. 5; minutes of PB meeting, April 20, 1983 (GD 100285), p. 5; minutes of PB/EB meeting, June 29, 1983 (GD 104061), p. 6; Edward Dew, "Did Suriname Switch?" *Caribbean Review,* vol. 12, no. 4 (Fall 1983), pp. 29–30. "Report of Mission to Moscow," p. 8; "Report on Trip to Antigua," unsigned, undated (GD 104366).

60. "Foreign Relations Report," undated general survey of PRG foreign relations, probably drafted about the middle of 1981 (GD unnumbered), p. 6; letter to Maurice Bishop from Humberto Ortega Saavedra, Minister of Defense of Nicaragua, dated February 19, 1981 (GD unnumbered); minutes of EB meeting, April 22, 1983 (GD 100297), p. 3.

61. "Foreign Relations Report" pp. 9–14; "Socialist International—An Assessment From Grenada's Perspective," undated, apparently drafted around 1981, (GD unnumbered); Memorandum to NJM leadership from "Comrade Whiteman," on the "Emergency S.I. Meeting in Panama," dated March 3, 1981 (GD unnumbered).

62. Minutes of CC meeting, January 13 and 15, 1982 (GD 104060), p. 2.

63. "U.S.-Grenada Relations," pp. 35–39.

64. *Ibid.,* pp. 39–40.

65. *Ibid.,* pp. 40–42; "personal and confidential" letter to Maurice Bishop from Ashley C. Taylor, LL.B., written from Ontario, Canada and dated August 21, 1979 (GD 002604); conversation with Lloyd Noel.

66. "PRG Statement on the Ortiz Affair: Desperate Effort Says Bishop," *Torchlight,* May 17, 1979, p. 1; "Ortiz Cables *Torchlight* Again," *ibid.,* p. 3; Sunshine, *Peaceful Rev,* p. 66; "U.S.-Grenada Relations," pp. 29–32.

67. *Grenada Newsletter,* June 21, 1980, pp. 1, 3; Sunshine, *Peaceful Rev,* pp. 67–68; "U.S.-Grenada Relations," pp. 53–54.

68. *Grenada Newsletter,* June 28, 1980, p. 1; "U.S.-Grenada Relations," pp. 55–56.

69. "International Military Forces Conduct Anti-Terrorist Exercises in Puerto Rico," report dated August 18, (1981) (GD 003334); minutes of extraordinary CC meetings, June 14–16, 1981 (GD unnumbered), p. 5; "U.S.-Grenada Relations," p. 80. Castro's "information" may have had some connection with an allegation later published in the *Washington Post* that "the CIA developed plans in the summer of 1981 to cause economic difficulty for Grenada in hopes of undermining the political control of Prime Minister Maurice Bishop," which plans had been scrubbed because of Senate opposition

(Patrick E. Tyler, "U.S. Tracks Cuban Aid to Grenada," *Washington Post*, February 27, 1983, p. A1).

70. "U.S.-Grenada Relations," pp. 38–39, Washington *Post*, September 1, 1979, p. C-1.

71. Text of President Reagan's speech to the National Association of Manufacturers at the Washington Hilton on March 10, 1983, as reported in a telex to St. George's (GD 003078); memo to "Permanent Secretary" (ministry not specified) from "Information Officer," dated March 11, (1983) (GD 002074).

72. "U.S.-Grenada Relations," pp. 63–68, 74.

73. *Ibid.*, pp. 68–69; "Brief Summary of Airport Studies Grenada 1954 to Present," undated (GD 001863).

74. *Ibid.*, pp. 71, 73; "Grenada: A Tiny Exporter of Revolution?" *Newsweek*, vol. 95, no. 13 (March 31, 1980), p. 44; diary of Liam James, entry for March 22, 1980 (GD unnumbered); Adams, "Grenada Update".

75. "U.S.-Grenada Relations," pp. 71–72.

76. *Ibid.*, p. 61.

77. Minutes of PB meeting, May 4, 1983 (GD 100766), p. 4; "Report on Visit of Prime Minister to U.S.A.," undated, submitted by "Comrade Ouwsu" (Liam James) (GD 103585); letter from Gail Reed, American wife of Cuban Ambassador to Grenada Julien Torres-Rizo, advising Maurice Bishop on tactics to use with the U.S. press during his tour (GD unnumbered); memo of W. Richard Jacobs, cited in "Problems of Communism," July–August, 1984, p. 21. It is interesting to note that the PRG kept a careful watch on American press reporting of Grenada at all times, and retained various American public relations firms to advise it on strategies to take with the U.S. press, public, and Congress.

78. "Line of March," pp. 9–10, 17–15.

79. *Ibid.*, pp. 42–46; notes from SG dated October 21, 1982.

80. "Line of March," p. 48; "Guidelines for the Strengthening and Building of the Party and Putting It on a Firmer Leninist Footing," undated, probably drafted about 1982 (GD 102066).

81. "Serious Workers Must Deal with Backward Bretheren," (GD unnumbered); "Links with the Masses," (GD 100897), pp. 1–3; "Council Document: 'Qualities of a Revolutionary'," (GD unnumbered). These documents do not appear to be of Grenadian origin, but were perhaps among the materials sent by the Workers' Party of Jamaica to help the NJM. They were found with collections of NJM ideological instruction materials.

82. "NJM's Work in Propaganda, 1973–1983," undated, found with materials from a Caribbean conference of leftist organizations held in August 1983 (GD 102973); "Draft Plan for Co-ordination of Party and State Propaganda," submitted to the NJM Political Bureau under cover of a memo dated September 5, 1983 on "Propaganda Among the Masses, July 24th–September 3rd" (GD 104061).

83. "Guidelines for Teaching in All Socialism Classes," Document No. 4 of the Training Seminar for Socialism and Crash Course Tutors, Monday, February 7, 1983 (GD 101951); "Study Guide for Marxist Leninist Philosophy," handwritten notes of unidentified student (GD 100469); "This is Imperialism" (GD 101985).

84. "Guidelines for Teaching in All Socialism Classes"; "Worker Education Tutors Seminar—Friday 9.9.83–Saturday 10.9.83" (GD 003196); "Worker Education Classes: Weekly Report No. 1," dated May 8, 1983 (GD unnumbered); "Worker Education Classes: Weekly Report No. 6," (June 13–17, 1983) (GD unnumbered); "Tutors Assessment," undated (GD 101260); memo to "All Government Ministeries, Departments, and State Enterprises" from Minister of National Mobilisation Selwyn Strachan, regarding Worker Education classes, undated (GD 002446); minutes of PB/EB meeting, August 24, 1983 (GD 104061), pp. 5–6; conversations with Margaret Dowe and Beverley Steele. Journalist George Worme publicized Strachan's letter throughout the Caribbean, thereby embarrassing the NJM leadership, and provoking a Political Bureau decision that Worme would be "dealt with" by calling in the Caribbean News Agency (CANA) and Radio Antilles to protest his reporting of several earlier stories (minutes of PB/EB meeting, August 17, 1983 [GD 104061]. p. 7).

85. "Guidelines for Broadening the Scope and Deepening the Context of the Involvement of the People in the Revolutionary Process," undated, signed by "E. J. Layne" (GD 101963).

86. "P.C.B. Work-Plan," undated, apparently drafted to guide work for the year 1983 (GD 100303); "Report for the Period June–August 1983," submitted to the NJM Political Bureau by the St. Patrick's PCB (GD 101262); conversation with a former NJM political commissar in charge of coordinating PCB activities in one of Grenada's parishes.

87. "Report of the Central Executive to First NYO Congress," December 12, 1981 (GD 102466), pp. 6, 11, 19–20; "Basic Training Course for NYO Recruitment," undated (GD 100470).

88. "N.W.O. Work-Plan—1983" (GD 100302), p. 1; "The Part the NWO must play in the Development of Women in Grenada, From 1983–89," undated (GD 101986); letter to Political Bureau from Phyllis Coard, Chairperson, Women's Committee, NJM, dated May 11, 1982 (GD 105657).

89. "Directive of the Minister of Defence and Interior for the Political Ideological and Academic Work in the Armed Forces," undated, probably drafted about late 1981 (GD 101957); "Directive from the Ministry of Defence on the Party Political Work in the PRAF," dated September 1983 (GD 101111).

90. Letter from Herbert Blaize to Prime Minister Bishop dated April 30, 1980 (GD 104259); "Draft Constitution of the State of Grenada," (GD 001684); conversation with Herbert Blaize.

91. Minutes of PB meeting, July 14, 1982 (GD 103998), p. 1; minutes of PB meeting May 18, 1983 (GD unnumbered), p. 5; Emmanuel, "Revolutionary Theory and Political Reality," p. 221.

92. Camille Ramnarace, "Ministry of National Mobilisation: A People's Ministry," news feature released by the Government Information Service on September 11, 1981 (GD 003274); "Draft Report to the Central Committee on the Party's Secretariat for the Period of January–June, 1983 (GD 102602), p. 3. The expediency for the NJM of Strachan's ministry is evident from minutes of a PB meeting on November 10, 1982 (GD unnumbered), in which it was agreed that the Dome, an important auditorium at Grand Anse Beach, "should be put under Party control through shifting it from under the Ministry of Education to that of Mobilisation," and that another building be studied for similar treatment.

93. "Progress Report of Commission No. 5," p. 3; notes of SG meeting dated January 6, 1983; "Guidelines for the Strengthening and Building of the Party," p. 3. Some notes in Bishop's handwriting, undated but apparently taken down sometime in 1983, suggest that a constitution and elections might have had to wait even longer, with the first draft of a constitution to be completed and submitted to a referendum in December 1986, the constitution to take effect in March 1987, presidential elections by about December 1989 and elections for a National Assembly by December 1990, in time for the Second Party Congress (GD 001899).

FIVE
Dissent, Decline and Collapse

The crackdown of October–November 1979 marked the beginning of serious disaffection from the NJM regime. The *Torchlight* closure and the waves of arrests that followed were intended to silence reaction and solidify the revolution. Instead they inaugurated a downward spiral of repression, resistance, NJM overreaction and more repression that reduced Grenada in four and a half years to a terrorized, divided society. In disgust, the people rejected the revolution, and the NJM in a fit of despair and recrimination destroyed itself.

The first vocal dissent came from the same groups on which the NJM had relied for support in its own campaign against Gairy. Both the GNP and the churches spoke out, albeit cautiously, against the government's actions in October 1979. When Bishop went on Radio Free Grenada on November 4, to solicit public suggestions on how to deal with the detainees, the churches responded again. In Bishop Charles's absence, Vicar General Cyril Lamontagne sent a letter on behalf of the Roman Catholic clergy to "humbly submit the following points": (1) that all citizens, whether charged with a crime or not, had human rights which must be respected for the good of all; (2) that treatment of alleged criminals should be strictly according to prevailing law; and (3) that suspects must be detained under humane conditions, and punished only when guilt was proven. "The credibility of the present Government of Grenada . . . requires that justice should be done and be seen to be done." Five days later on November 14, the Conference of Churches in Grenada (CCG) followed up with an appeal for relief of specific hardships suffered by a number of detainees.

Reactions also poured in from the general public. Many of these were supportive of the government. Many accepted the official claim that the "counter-revolutionaries" were out to kill the NJM leaders and overthrow the revolution on behalf of Gairy and his "imperialist backers." Some called for summary execution of the culprits as an example, while others asked for moderation. There were also a number of unsigned letters warning Bishop that the wrath of God would continue to pursue him unless he abandoned the evil path on which he had embarked.[1]

The NJM leaders feared the churches. Grenadians are deeply religious, at least 80 percent being confirmed believers according to a 1982 study. The majority of these—about 60 per cent—are Roman Catholics, followed closely by Anglicans, and then a number of smaller demoninations including Methodists, Presbyterians, and some "non-traditional" churches like Seventh Day Adventists and Jehovah's Witnesses, which had sprung up since World War II. Add the fact that education in Grenada had long been dominated by religious schools, and the social influence of the churches was enormous. For that very reason, the churches had proven a powerful ally against Gairy in the early 1970s. They had played a key role in the Committee of 22 and in the human-rights campaigns of that period. Gairy's corruption and brutality, as well as his ham-handed efforts to pervert religion to his own political ends, had won him the enmity of the clergy (most of whom were non-Grenadians). Some had gone so far as to support the NJM, notably one or two Dominican friars who were politically inclined and were encouraged by the good Catholic upbringing of Bishop and his fellow leaders.[2] The Dominicans stayed on as advisors for a while after the NJM took power, and were useful as a symbol of apparent church support for the new regime. And, despite the events of October–November 1979, overall the churches remained supportive for a time, especially of the PRG's social and economic development programs.

Dissatisfaction started to show itself among the clergy by early 1980, as the direction of the PRG's policies became clearer. A top-secret government security report of February 11, 1980, alleged that some Catholic priests, including one of the Dominicans, were circulating political tracts "aimed at showing that communism is atheistic and should be feared and that our party is communist." CCG meetings with Prime Minister Bishop achieved no progress on human rights issues, and became strained. When the Roman Catholic church published a new newspaper, the *Catholic Focus*, in February 1980, the PRG promptly closed it down, claiming it violated the *"Torchlight* law" forbidding any individual to own more than 4 per cent of a newspaper.[3]

At that point, a stroke of luck gave the NJM a chance to square off with the churches on its own terms. A Grenadian who had been fired from a position as a typist for some Dominican friars in Trinidad managed to retain a copy of a letter sent from the friars in Trinidad to their brothers in the UK. He passed this copy to Maurice Bishop. The letter, in its original form, noted that "within Grenada, whatever political ideas may be entertained by the handful of people responsible for the PRG are becoming submerged under a massive Cuban influence. Cuba, Angola, Viet-Nam and Kampuchea are now upheld as the models of development of a free Third World State." The friars suspected that the NJM intended to reduce the church to an "irrelevant organization for children and old people." They recommended that some of the brethren in England who were interested in a Christian-Marxist dialogue, and who "are probably better-read in modern Marxist ideology than any of the members of the PRG," be sent to Grenada. This would afford them "an opportunity to preach the gospel in a predominantly Marxist oriented society while, at the same time, cooperating and assisting in the efforts to construct a just, humane society."[4]

In Bishop's hands, this letter became the infamous "Priests' Plot." In a radio address on February 15, 1980, Bishop reminded his listeners of the counter-revolutionary plot of the previous

November, and continued, "tonight I want to present to you concrete evidence of counter-revolutionary activities by a few individuals seeking to use the church to create just such confusion and disharmony." With the help of a few selected phrases from the letter, which he interpreted for his audience, he explained that a "tiny minority of foreign priests," although obviously aware of the revolution's popularity and of the government's efforts to cooperate with the church, had "laid careful plans to sabotage the revolution" by making it appear to be against religion. This, he explained, was precisely the sort of tactic used by the CIA. Bishop went on to quote from the February 11 security report (with some editorial changes) to demonstrate that political tracts were already being circulated "to distort the policies, program, and objectives of the NJM . . . so as to make them appear as communistic. . . . " Meanwhile, one or two priests had also been attacking the revolution in sermons and private conversations.[5]

Bishop said he accepted the word of Bishop Charles that he and most of his clergy were ignorant of this "sinister plan." He also reiterated the PRG's "fullest commitment to freedom of worship and religion." "But by the same token," he warned, "we are not prepared to allow the church or elements within the church . . . to use their influence and standing as religious leaders to engage in counter-revolutionary activities against the interests of the people." The government-controlled media picked up the major themes of Bishop's attack and made them even more explicit, printing letters, comments, and editorials referring to the "CIA priests." The *Free West Indian* ran a long poem entitled "Devil Priest, Evil Beast." Bishop Charles called the Prime Minister's charges "absurd." Nonetheless, the NJM's warning-shot helped quiet some criticism of the regime from the pulpit, particularly among the Dominicans, and led the church to be more circumspect in its activities in the future.[6]

The first round with the church had ended in a draw. But opposition was bubbling up again among former NJM supporters, including many who had been swept up in the arrests of late 1979. Some of these, like Howard University professor Stanley Cyrus, who was arrested during a visit to Grenada, left the country and organized emigré resistance movements in the U.S. and Trinidad. Others like Attorney General Lloyd Noel and Tillman Thomas, Bishop's former legal partner, quit the government and bided their time, waiting for an opportunity to organize some effective opposition. Still others were unwilling to wait, and moved to action.

THE "ULTRA-LEFTISTS"

On February 13, 1980, Kenneth "Buck" Budhlall and a few supporters—revolutionary idealists who felt betrayed by the PRG—occupied the River Antoine Estate near their home in Tivoli, St. Patrick's (on the northern tip of the island). Ostensibly this was an exercise in proletarian democracy: Budhlall had persuaded the workers they could run the estate as a cooperative and reap the fruits of their labor themselves. In fact, it was a calculated act of rebellion, coordinated with anti-PRG resolutions passed in the Tivoli area the same day, accusing Bishop and company of having sold out to the bourgeoisie. "Buck" Budhlall had decided to force the NJM out into the open: to create a popular cause that would compel the regime either to support it and yield the initiative to the grassroots leaders again, or (as Budhlall expected), to crush the move and restore control to the landowners, thereby revealing its betrayal of the people.

The PRG smelled the trap. Senior police officials went out to negotiate with the Budhlall group and quietly persuaded them to turn the keys to the estate over to the owners (the prominent De Gale family, one of whom had been a recent Governor General of Grenada). Bishop called in Lyden Ramdhanny, a cousin of the Budhlalls, to mediate. "Buck," however, wouldn't budge, and continued to make impossible demands on behalf of the estate workers. Finally, after the Budhlall group instituted a work slowdown on the estate and gave an interview to journalist Alister Hughes, the PRG lost patience. On April 25, the day after the interview, the government moved in and began arresting the boys from Tivoli. "Buck" Budhlall and Evan Bhola, another leader of the group, went into hiding but were captured two weeks later.[7]

The ferment, however, went on. In a May Day speech, Bishop accused the Tivoli dissidents of being "ultra-leftists" who endangered the revolution. The dissidents replied with anti-PRG demonstrations on May 4th and 8th, to which the government in turn responded with its own demonstration in Grenville. Meanwhile the anti-government pamphleteering continued, and took a darker tone. Stran Phillip, seething about the influx of Cubans and the autocratic control of the old Bureau leaders, issued a tract declaring:

> Free Grenada is just a joke. Now we are in slavery. . . . Right at this time more than ten thousand (10,000) Cubans are waiting for evacuation from the Socialist Block. Is this what Grenadians want? I thought they would develop their own system, one suited for Grenada, and not swallow another's 'hook, line and sinker.'

Recounting his many sacrifices for the revolution, Phillip continued,

> Brothers and Sisters I hope you understand why I'm willing to shed my blood for you. Don't laugh, because tomorrow it's yours.[8]

Kennedy Budhlall, who had originally rejected his brothers' position, was now also preparing to break with the NJM. In early 1980, Kennedy was still the PRA commander at Pearls Airport and had a strong personal following in the army. He and the other Budhlalls were also close to dissident "Rastas" and Muslims, both in Tivoli and beyond. These were socially marginal types, mostly young, who had supported the revolution because they disliked Gairy and were given to understand that an NJM government would not interfere with them or their customs, including use of marijuana. When the PRG began to crack down on these "lumpen elements" (as party leaders called them) the Rastas and Muslims drew together in common cause with the old JEWEL leaders.

Kennedy Budhlall had already confronted Bishop once, calling him aside during a rally in late 1979 and warning him that the Coards were plotting to take over the NJM. The Coards, he argued, were removing loyal Bishop supporters (like himself) and putting their own people in positions of power. Kennedy threatened to leave the party if this trend went on.

By about April 1980, under pressure from friends who were pleading with him to do something to restrain the government, Kennedy finally decided "to put a stop to the PRG." He met with Stran Phillip and others of like mind, and began preparing his move. But Bishop got wind of the plot. He removed Budhlall from command at the airport in time to forestall an armed rebellion—but not in time to prevent Budhlall and his supporters from making off with some guns and distributing them to supporters in the Mt. Rich-Tivoli area. When Budhlall failed to show up the next week for a new assignment in the Prime Minister's office (where he could be watched), the PRA went to get him. On May 29, he joined the detainees in Richmond Hill Prison.[9]

Three weeks later, Queen's Park was bombed. A detachment of People's Revolutionary Army troops was immediately dispatched to Stran Phillip's home in Mt. Airy outside St. George's. There they found Phillip and gunned him down. His girlfriend later claimed that he had surrendered to the troops after receiving a single bullet wound in the leg. The coroner's report counted nineteen bullet wounds in the body, and one of the two policeman who went to the scene afterward described Phillip as having been "brutally murdered." Ralph Thompson, a tough character who had defied Gairy's police and sold *The New JEWEL* openly on the streets of St. George's in the party's opposition years, was also arrested that day and later died in prison. On July 2 the PRA captured three more of the Budhlall brothers. Other suspects were harder to track down. A sporadic guerrilla campaign of bombings, ambushes, and shootouts between the PRA and Muslim or Rasta insurgents of the so-called "Budhlall Gang" dragged on throughout 1980.[10]

The activities of the Budhlalls and their fellow sympathizers never seriously threatened the NJM's hold on power (except possibly in the Queen's Park bombing itself). But they had a deeply sobering effect on the regime. Beginning with Bishop's speech on June 19, the PRG tried to link the armed attacks in Grenada to the external forces of "imperialism." At the trial for the Queen's Park bombing the PRG produced dubious "evidence" that the bomb incorporated sophisticated technology supplied from abroad. Doubtless the NJM leaders were themselves convinced that the U.S. was involved. But they also began to realize they had bitter enemies within the island. That realization compounded their growing suspicion of and alienation from the Grenadian people, and led them down a path that earned them still more enemies.

Security measures and surveillance of the general population were increased. Off-hand remarks in a bar or a denunciation by someone's former girlfriend or neighbor could bring arrest and interrogation. The Ministry of the Interior in Havana sent specialists to help with security work. Bishop, in an October 5th address to the nation, denounced "rumour mongering," as a subversive activity aimed at destabilizing the revolution, and called upon Grenadians to report anyone involved in such activity to the security forces. At about the same time, the PRG passed a Terrorism Prevention Law prescribing death or a long prison term for anyone found guilty of setting off a bomb or even possessing "an explosive substance." By the terms of this law, a person arrested on such a charge was guilty until proven innocent.[11]

A number of suspects picked up on suspicion of terrorist activities in summer 1980 were brutalized so badly by PRA interrogators that the government itself launched an investigation. Testimony taken at that time from over 20 witnesses, (including a physician), accused Major Leon "Bogo" Cornwall, Lieutenant Cecil Prime, Lieutenant (later Captain) Lester Redhead, Captain (later Lieutenant Colonel) Ewart Layne, and other PRA soldiers of kicking, beating, branding, shooting and otherwise torturing suspects rounded up in the Mt. Rich-Tivoli area in an effort to extract information about the whereabouts of the "Budhlall Gang." Some of this mistreatment resulted in permanent injuries.[12]

The regime was deeply distrustful of the police, and not without reason. A large number of policemen were resentful over their low pay, loss of status to the PRA, and perhaps most of all, the arrest and mistreatment of some of their colleagues as "counter-revolutionaries" in 1979. The police were disarmed after the March 13 coup, and the Police Commissioner and one of his two deputies were replaced by NJM appointees. Policemen were ordered off the streets during the curfews imposed, to cover the arrival of Cuban arms shipments and other secret business. During a curfew after the Queen's Park bombing, Deputy Commissioner Luckey Bernard (not a PRG appointee) ventured out after dark and was shot and left for dead by PRA troops—who had recognized him—when he failed to get out of his car as ordered. PRA officers could and did summarily dismiss police investigators from a case when they felt so inclined. In fact, the PRG conducted repeated investigations of the police and finally subordinated the entire Grenada Police Service to the Army command. New police recruits were trained in Cuba and promoted quickly over the heads of the Gairy-era veterans. Such measures only deepened the animosities of the old guard. With obvious passion Luckey Bernard confided to U.S. Embassy officers his disdain for the "young upstarts" of the NJM, who "must change or they must be *made* to change."[13]

THE "GANG OF 26"

As the summer of 1981 approached, in several apparently unrelated events, the NJM read the signs of another major conspiracy. CBS News in the United States ran a three-part, prime-time exposé on mistreatment of political detainees in Grenada, entitled "Prisoner in a Police State." The Political Bureau dispatched Kenrick Radix to New York to organize protest rallies in response to this "propaganda."

Shortly afterward, party leaders noticed that the Rastas were becoming active. Rasta groups were convening for suspicious gatherings called "Nya Bingis." Desmond Trotter, a radical from Dominica whom Bishop had defended in a celebrated court case in the mid-1970's, was meeting with Rasta leaders and "bad talking" the PRG and the Cubans. In a meeting with Bishop in early June, Trotter and a delegation of 14 Rastas presented a four-page list of demands, including a call for release of some detainees. (Phyllis Coard proposed handling the Rastas by some combination of "ideological struggle," employment on road work or state farms, and prison farms.)[14]

Then a bombshell hit. A group of 26 prominent Grenadians formed a company called Spice Isle Printers, Ltd., and published the first issue of a new newspaper, the *Grenadian Voice*. In a sense, the *Voice* was a middle-class effort to do what the rural radicals had attempted to do with the River Antoine seizure: force the NJM regime to show its true colors. Convinced that the regime's purpose in closing the *Torchlight* and the *Catholic Focus* had been nothing less than the complete and permanent elimination of a free press, Leslie Pierre, Lloyd Noel, Alistair Hughes and the 23 others set out to create a test case. They issued a politically innocuous newspaper that conformed scrupulously to all existing laws, including People's Law No. 81 of 1979, the "*Torchlight* law," which had been used to justify closing down the earlier two publications. They fully expected the PRG to expose itself by closing the *Voice* immediately as well, regardless of legalities. They did not, however, expect the ferocity of the PRG's response.[15]

Through contacts with some of the *Voice* shareholders, the American Embassy in Bridgetown had gotten wind of the project and had passed the word back to Washington. When Radix stopped by the State Department en route to New York, American officials mentioned to him their interest in an "independent newspaper" to be started in Grenada. An Embassy official visiting Grenada had also tried to sound out an employee in the official PRG media about the government's likely response to such a venture. This was enough evidence to persuade the hardliners in the NJM Central Committee that the *Voice* was merely the leading edge of a massive CIA plot that somehow included the Rastas and the other dissidents.

At an extraordinary Central Committee meeting of June 14–16, 1981, Bernard Coard moved to strike the prearranged agenda and focus on one issue: "The Present Threat of Counter-Revolution." The bourgeoisie had been "under firm manners" until recently, Coard maintained. But now that they had the backing of the Reagan administration to overthrow the PRG, they were starting to make their move. The 26 shareholders of the *Voice* were the nucleus of a party to be launched "this month." The situation called for drastic measures: Coard, looking at the situation in class terms, proposed "full scale nationalization of the banks, the large merchant houses and the land belonging to all the National Farmers Union members [large farmers] by mid-day on Friday, June 19th."[16] Other Central Committee members, including Bishop, balked at such an extreme move for fear of the popular reaction it might provoke. But all agreed that radical steps were necessary. Finally the Central Committee agreed to the following steps:

- Sister Coard was to write a pamphlet pointing out that every newspaper represents a class, therefore there is no such thing as an "independent" newspaper;
- George Louison would take a message from Bishop to Castro, and would ask Trevor Munroe to send two comrades from Jamaica to help with propaganda;
- The second issue of the *Voice* would be seized by security forces on Thursday night, June 18;
- The *"Torchlight* Law" would be amended to permit no new newspapers until a media policy was adopted;
- Key Rasta leaders were to be arrested, and Desmond Trotter picked up and deported;
- A letter was to be sent to Ronald Reagan giving him a 90-day ultimatum to restore good relations with Grenada, or face the consequences;
- A rally would be held on June 19, the first anniversary of the Queen's Park bombing, with the theme "The Revolution Must Be Respected," and this slogan was to be painted in front of the businesses and homes of the 26.[17]

The Central Committee's resolutions were carried out. On June 19, Bishop was at his rhetorical best. Recalling for the crowd assembled at Queen's Park the tragedy of the previous year, he declared that:

Our people today have reason to feel proud and confident. Those who have to be concerned today are not our dead heroes and martyrs, not those who imperialism killed; those people who have

135

to stand and tremble in their boots are imperialism itself and the local counter-revolutionaries and the local reactionaries, the local Committee of Twenty-Six.

These elements, Bishop explained, had chosen now to "crawl out from under their beds" and try to confuse the people, pretending to be interested in freedom of the press. What they really meant was their own freedom as a small minority to dominate the media, ignoring matters of real interest to the people, such as the achievements of the revolution, and instead spreading slander and rubbish. The enemy, though, was "not just some parisites who are running what they call the *Grenadian Voice*," but rather "the full fury of the organized CIA, which has made up its mind in the clearest possible way that it is out to overthrow our revolution, and it has told these local elements, these parasites, that they can have the fullest and firmest backing of imperialism in their plan to overthrow the revolution." After attacking some of the leaders of the 26 personally, Bishop finally warned:

> This is a revolution, we live in a revolutionary Grenada. . . . there is a revolutionary legality, and they will have to abide by the laws of the revolution.
>
> When the revolution speaks, it must be heard, listened to. Whatever the revolution decrees, it must be obeyed; when the revolution commands, it must be carried out; when the revolution talks, no parasite must bark in their corner. . . . The revolution must be respected.[18]

On July 10, party leaders resolved to arrest Leslie Pierre, Stanley Roberts, Lloyd Noel and Tillman Thomas, and to confiscate their businesses. The homes of several others of the 26 were to be searched for weapons. Alistair Hughes got off with a warning, probably because his international reputation made it too politically costly to jail him.

At the same time the PRG began rounding up the Rastas. The Central Committee had concluded that the Rastas were about to "go on the offensive" in the northern part of the island, but worried that there wasn't enough room in the prison to hold all of them. Vince Noel suggested that "the army should prepare a programme for the Rastas who will be picked up—wake up time, eat time, books, films, pacifying music, etc.—a rigid programme." Bishop, though, declared himself "totally against taking up 300 of them and cutting their hair as was proposed." Cuban Ambassador Torres-Rizo counseled caution, lest Grenada be isolated regionally and internationally, and suggested waiting to let the Rastas make the first move, so as to "legitimise" the PRG's measures. Nevertheless, the party proceeded to draw up a list of Rasta leaders to be arrested and to construct a detention camp at Hope Vale to hold 300 people. The roundups began in July 1981, and for the duration of the PRG regime large numbers of Rastas were held at Hope Vale and other camps under squalid conditions, forced to wear uniforms and work in the fields, growing food for the People's Revolutionary Army.[19]

In its final meeting of 1981, the Central Committee comrades congratulated themselves on having dealt firmly with the "Gang of 26" and successfully crushed the counter-revolution. The moves against the Rastas had not been too unpopular. The Rastas themselves were regarded by much of established society as dangerous riffraff, and the leaders had hopes that decent young people would benefit from the removal of their mischievous influence. By 1982, disenchantment with the regime was spreading fast, but all the regimes most capable opponents had been crushed—except for the church.[20]

ATTACK ON THE CHURCH

After the "Priests' Plot" incident of February 1980, relations between the churches and the government were uneasy, but not antagonistic. The PRG strove to hold the church "under manners," though, by encouraging visits from Marxist "liberation" theologians, especially from Nicaragua, and cultivating the left wing of the Caribbean Conference of Churches (CCC) as a counterweight to the local Conference of Churches in Grenada. Early in the summer of 1981 Maurice Bishop met with a Reverend Lett, a left-wing leader of the CCC in Antigua. Lett had information.

He urged Bishop to take active steps against any counter-revolutionary activity from the church in Grenada, because "the progressive church in the region is under serious pressure in that there is a great chance of the reactionaries taking power in the upcoming elections for the CCC."[21]

In the light of this information, plus some other recent activities of Bishop Charles that the PRG regarded with suspicion, such as an alleged "clandestine meeting" with the Venezuelan OAS Ambassador, party leaders concluded that the church might well be preparing a "major thrust against the Revolution." Selwyn Strachan felt that Bishop Charles should be called in for a strong warning; while Bishop and Whiteman offered to contact other church figures whom they thought they could influence, including Luckey Bernard. The Political Bureau also agreed to lodge a complaint with Bishop Charles's superiors. But most importantly, it agreed to seek advice from the Cubans on how to manage the church.[22]

Little was done for almost a year. The "Gang of 26" affair, the roundup of the Rastas, and the invasion scare of August 1981 occupied the NJM's attention, and church relations remained relatively quiescent. In summer 1982, though, Aurelio Alonso Tejada arrived from Cuba to conduct a thorough analysis of the religious situation in Grenada. Tejada concluded that the attitude of the Grenadian churches, particularly the Roman Catholic church, was in harmony with the anti-PRG campaigns conducted by "reactionary governments in the Caribbean," as well as with a pastoral issued by the Caribbean Catholic bishops earlier that year. That pastoral denounced violence, maintained that a coup did not legitimize a government (clearly a slap at the PRG) and emphasized the pre-eminent rights of the individual. Moreover, it contained references to "noxious foreign influences" threatening the region and "attempts to impose the ideology of atheistic Marxism on our peoples," an implicit warning to the PRG.[23]

Under the banner of a human-rights campaign, the Caribbean reaction had been trying, in Tejada's opinion, to enlist the churches as an opposition force against the PRG. Tejada recommended several steps that might be taken to minimize the danger of any church-based opposition. The NJM should appoint a comrade to monitor church activities, and send him to Cuba for training. A Register of Associations should be established with legal authority to compile records on the membership, meeting places, activities and financing of all church and social groups. The schools should be taken out of church control. The NJM should promote contacts with clergymen and members of churches in Nicaragua and "other Latin American circles linked to the theology of liberation." The NJM should try to influence the CCG through the more left-leaning elements of the CCC (of which Cuban churches were members). Finally, the NJM, the Cuban Communist Party, and the FSLN of Nicaragua should exchange information and hold regular strategy discussions.[24]

In response to Tejada's suggestions, the NJM delegated Michael "Chicken" Roberts, a senior security officer, to investigate the churches. Roberts focused on recruiting agents within the principal denominations—Roman Catholics, Anglicans, and Methodists—to inform him about their internal structure and thinking. In a March 15, 1983, report he concluded that the Roman Catholic Church, supported to some degree by the Anglicans and others, was "gearing up for confrontation with the government."[25]

The crisis, as the NJM saw it, had begun to brew toward the end of 1982. On December 23 a Methodist minister named Lettson had been deported by the PRG for refusing to perform a memorial service for two heroes of the NJM pantheon, Cacademo Grant and Theophilus Marryshow. The following day, Christmas Eve, Archdeacon Huggins had warned his congregation at St. George's Church to guard their freedom of worship jealously, otherwise they might lose it in the coming year. On January 2, in an address to the St. Vincent De Paul Society, Bishop Charles had said (according to Roberts) that the church was now facing its greatest challenge, and there would be attempts to crush the church in 1983. The Bishop had also begun reorganizing the Catholic youth organizations, allegedly to ensure their control by "reactionary elements." The Roman Catholics had imported over 4,000 copies of the Jerusalem Bible, written in simple English that the masses could understand. This suggested to Roberts that the Church was girding itself for the ideological struggle by revolutionizing its "main ideological weapon—the bible."[26]

Michael Roberts's findings were confirmed and reinforced in a July 1983 report by Major Keith Roberts, PRG head of security. The report noted as well that the smaller denominations seemed to be involved in a "frenzied drive to win new members" through open-air crusades and house-to-house visits. The Anglican Church, too, had started to reorganize its youth groups, and the Anglicans and Catholics had joined together for the first time in a Corpus Christi procession. The NJM found these developments highly alarming, particularly in view of "the weakness in all our mass organizations and, therefore, our influence over the masses." A Central Committee meeting had identified the "church issue" as one of the two problems, along with land reform, that could lead to the collapse of the revolution. As a result of Roberts's report, the Central Committee authorized renewed efforts to implement Tejada's earlier suggestions, plus a few others. Religious head-teachers were purged from the schools and mandatory political education was installed. The NJM also cut back drastically on religious programs broadcast by Radio Free Grenada. Roberts arranged to have the movements of church leaders watched, and their phones tapped. Bishop considered starting a "progressive church," a tactic the Sandinistas were employing in Nicaragua.[27]

Despite the party's best efforts, the influence of the churches was clearly on the rise during 1983, while NJM support was falling off just as sharply. Central Committee members lamented at a September 1983 meeting that the "church is winning people back." Fifty people had been baptized after a recent crusade in St. Patrick's, for example. The "Church is now using our tactics . . . and picking up our fall-out."[28]

The rise in church membership was but one of many symptoms of an overall decline in the regime's popularity. But the NJM, alert as it was to "plots," did not realize how generally unpopular it had become until the last months of its existence. By then, popular disaffection had reached crisis proportions as evidenced by the PRG's inability to mobilize the people against the alleged invasion threat of March 1983. Internal intelligence reports revealed that "about 50% to 70% do not believe in the threat," "the mood of the militia is low," "the mood of the mobilizers is low," and so on. One analysis noted that "the degree of alienation of the party from the masses is really frightening, to the extent that many party comrades were seriously intimidated by the mere idea of house-to-house visits among the masses."[29]

DISENCHANTMENT AND DISORGANIZATION

Though the revolution's unpopularity may have shocked its leaders, in the space of four years the PRG had given most Grenadians some reason to resent its rule. The issue of the detainees was one major grievance. The number of people incarcerated in Richmond Hill Prison varied with sporadic waves of arrests and releases, but reached 183 in January 1982. Approximately one Grenadian in every 500 was in prison—not counting the 300 or so Rastas at Hope Vale. By some estimates nearly one Grenadian out of 100 had been detained at one time or another by the time the PRG fell in 1983. Reasons for detention included anything from active opposition, to an unguarded remark, association with or proximity to known subversives, or mistaken identity.[30]

Conditions of confinement varied. Some prisoners, particularly some of those arrested for "counter-revolutionary plots" in 1979–1980 were taken to PRA Headquarters at Fort Rupert and tortured. The torture included beatings, brandings, long periods of exposure in the hot sun, mock executions, and a variety of other crude punishments. Once a prisoner was sent to Richmond Hill he usually got better treatment, although beatings, occasional shootings, and various forms of harassment also occurred there. Food and sanitation were poor, most prisoners had no blankets, and guards occasionally took away books and radios from the detainees or cut off food supplements sent by relatives and church groups. A prison report for 1982 indicated that two prisoners had died in custody that year. Some people were kept in detention for the entire reign of the PRG without trial; others were tried and convicted under the Terrorism Prevention Law, but were held even after their sentence expired.[31]

Protests from human-rights organizations such as the International Red Cross and Amnesty International generally received no reply. The PRG did draft one letter to the British section of Amnesty International, advising that replying to such a large volume of correspondence was "beyond the capacity of Grenada's small public service," but that Amnesty could rest assured that "all detainees are in comfortable and healthy accommodation and receiving good nourishing foods." Unfortunately the "unholy alliance between the American CIA and reactionary and mercenary local elements" required the PRG to continue detaining some suspects, but the government looked forward to the day when this would no longer be necessary. In the meantime, Amnesty's "campaign of pressure against Grenada" was "entirely unjustified," and the organization would do well to devote its energies to freeing persons unjustly imprisoned by truly repressive regimes like South Africa and Chile.[32]

The protests within Grenada were also mainly ignored. Bishop's files contained numerous letters from family members pleading for the release of husbands or fathers arrested and held for no apparent reason, and whose absence was a source of financial as well as psychological hardship to their dependents. Even Grenadians who were not touched directly suffered from the atmosphere of terror created by constant surveillance and the fear of arrest. One farmer in St. Patrick's recalled that he had welcomed the NJM coup because Gairy's "Green Beasts" were always reporting on people who spoke against the government, but before long the NJM had paid-informers and militia doing the same work, only more thoroughly. Bernard Coard was especially fond of reminding people that there was "plenty of room up on the hill."[33]

The flood of foreigners into Grenada, especially Cubans, was another sore point. While many of the Cuban doctors and teachers who came to Grenada were, as one Grenadian put it, "beautiful people," the airport construction workers and political-military advisors were cut from a different cloth. NJM leaders were constantly concerned about frictions and resentments between Grenadians and Cubans at the airport. And people constantly complained that the airport project was providing jobs for hundreds of Cubans, but hardly any Grenadians. Moreover, the government was constantly seizing vacant houses to accommodate its many foreign workers and advisors. Grenadians living overseas would sometimes pay relatives to occupy their homes to keep them from being seized.

Even more than the foreigners themselves, though, people resented and feared what they stood for, and seemed to foreshadow. Many Grenadians had lived and worked in Cuba before 1959, had acquired property or small businesses, and then had returned home penniless after Castro took power and expropriated them. Grenadians did not want a Cuban-style revolution — much less a Soviet-style one. Their fears were thus redoubled when Soviets began to arrive in 1983 as diplomatic staff at the new Soviet Embassy or as science teachers in the schools.[34]

Not least of all, Grenadians resented the constant bombardment of propaganda, especially anti-American propaganda. There was scarcely a family in Grenada that did not have a relative living in New York or Boston whose remittances to those back home made life a little easier, and often ensured a merry Christmas instead of a meager one. Grenadians knew America and Americans first hand, and many dreamed of emigrating there or to Canada or England. Not that the NJM's diatribes about "imperialism" fell on totally deaf ears: Grenadians harbored residual animosities over the historical exploitation of black people by the colonial powers and over reports of persistant racism. The New JEWEL leaders manipulated these feelings skillfully at first. Eventually, however, they overplayed their hand. NJM propaganda was crude, often clumsy, and over time it bore less and less of a relationship to reality.[35]

Despite glowing reports of economic progress and major development projects, after the first few months roads were no longer being built, markets did not improve, prices and taxes rose, living standards declined, and workers began to be laid off. A new harbor promised for Carriacou was never completed, while PRG projects to repair the road and telephone systems there led to even worse roads, and a total collapse of telephone service. New generators promised for the power company didn't arrive, so that while electricity rates went steadily up, service went just as steadily down. Farmers resented the NJM's land-reform policy, too. They didn't quite understand what the NJM was trying to do, but they recalled that Bishop and the other party leaders had always attacked Gairy for "stealing land." When the NJM came to power they didn't give the land back as they said they would; rather they "stole more land."[36]

The party's reaction was to call for more propaganda, more mobilization, tighter discipline, greater recruitment efforts for mass organizations, etc. But the people did not respond. Parish Coordinating Body reports for mid-1983 complained of the "low mood" among the people, poor attendance at meetings, and the masses' "alienation from the party." A report from St. Andrews noted that:

> By far, the areas of greatest concern in this period must be the work of the youths, farmers, women. The political work among the mass organizations seems non-existent as can be observed by the low participation and drop in membership within these organizations, and their low participation generally in the Programmes of the Revolution.

By late 1982 about 80 percent of NYO groups had collapsed. Party leaders made a major effort and managed to improve this situation slightly by 1983, but a report in July of that year concluded that "the mood is still very low among our youth."[37]

Attendance at mass rallies grew embarrassingly meager: Unison Whiteman told a Central Committee meeting on September 14 that a recent "Bolivar Day" rally had turned out 10 Grenadians; while a "Vietnam/Peace Day" rally had produced 20 plus a contingent of the PRA. A Canadian working in Grenada recalled visiting one major rally at Queen's Park and seeing crowds of enthusiastic European and North American leftists cheering in the stands, while a few listless Grenadians played dominos and drank rum on the field. In December 1982, the leadership decided to hold a "scaled down" March 13th celebration the next year, with small local gatherings, some military parades, and no international guests.[38]

The popular mood was also evident from comments made in "Worker Education Classes," and recorded faithfully in the reports of the socialism tutors. One tutor observed in May 1983 that "there is a definite . . . section who are openly hostile to the Revo, to the Soviet Union and to a 'Non Parliamentary Path,'" and offered a sample of student opinion: "Who is the aggressor — Grenada or the U.S.? I never hear Reagan cuss Maurice like how Maurice cuss Reagan"; "Leave us in Grenada as we are, we don't want no 'Ism'"; "Does the Soviet Union trade in Foreign Exchange or only barter?" One worker allegedly did not like the previous tutor because he was "'Biased' and one-sided in calling U.S.A. imperialist and not the U.S.S.R." Comments from other classes included: "You say the Soviet Union is for peace, but look how a Soviet Plane just shoot down and kill two hundred and sixty (260) innocent civilians"; "If Cuba is so free, why is it I know a man in Fontenoy used to live in Cuba and had to come back to Grenada with only his shirt on his back after working twenty (20) years?"; "Why are so many foreigners working in the country, and why are they given the best jobs and better pay than Grenadians?" and "Where is govt. getting all the arms? Why is government having relations with those who cannot help us?"[39]

Incredibly, this rising tide of animosity never touched Maurice Bishop. Most NJM leaders acquired a reputation for being haughty and officious once they attained status as government ministers and army officers. But Bishop always remained easygoing and approachable, with an unself-conscious dignity that one acquaintance described as "West Indian macho." Handsome, virile, and yet somehow gentle, he was the image of all the revolution was supposed to be. People felt they could confide in him, and would write to him asking help with all sorts of problems. He also received a number of amorous letters from women, some of them apparently strangers.

The paradox in popular feelings toward the revolution on the one hand, and its leader on the other, reflects a paradox in Bishop himself. He was a man of many contradictions who succeeded in being all things to all people because of the ambiguities in his own nature. Raised by devout Catholic parents, he was beyond doubt a committed Marxist in his own mind. He believed in the revolution and had a key role in formulating its policies. On the other hand he was a genuine nationalist and anti-colonialist who, in recruiting Lyden Ramdhanny for the cause, confided with every appearance of genuine conviction that he didn't believe Marxism-Leninism could be applied in its entirety to a West Indian society. When others in the Central Committee were convinced of counter-revolutionary threats and resolved to take drastic action, Bishop hesitated, temporized, and looked for a less radical solution. Yet in his rhetoric he was uncompromisingly radical, and he never failed to publicly defend actions that were taken by party leaders in his absence or against his better judgment. Above all, he believed in maintaining a united front.

These characteristics earned him a reputation among his colleagues for "vacillating leadership." He was a man of vaulting ideals but little patience with details. His style of leadership was visceral, highly personal, and (as Coard would have said) *undisciplined*. But whatever his failings in Marxist terms, the Grenadian people loved Bishop's personal approach to politics as they had Gairy's. In a sense they were so loyal to Maurice Bishop because he was so unlike his revolution. Several months after the intervention and Bishop's death, many Grenadians who would talk eagerly about anything else concerning the revolution, found themselves unable to speak about Bishop. As one woman, choked with emotion, put it, "I always loved Maurice—it's so hard to believe he was selling us out."[40]

Bernard Coard was Bishop's diametric opposite. If Bishop was what the people had hoped the revolution would be, Coard was what they feared it had become. Coard could be witty and affable when the occasion called for it. He even managed to impress some visiting journalists as less of a rigid ideologue than the more straightforward Bishop. He was also a man with whom one could reason: Ramdhanny recalls, for example, that Coard would argue rationally and without rancor for hours to bring a respected colleague around to his views. Behind this civil exterior, however, lay a keen and calculating mind backed by an iron will, and a dedication to Marxist-Leninist "principle" that left little room for petit-bourgeois scruples. He was ambitious and, to a certain degree, brutal. This aspect of his nature earned him the hostility of the mass of Grenadians. Among his colleagues in the

PRG, though, Coard was respected as a hard-working, efficient manager untouched by any suspicion of the corruption that had darkened the reputations of some other NJM leaders. He was, in short, a model Marxist.

For years people tried to warn Bishop that Coard was a danger, but Bishop refused to listen. He simply would not discuss the subject, even with his family. Bishop regarded Coard's theoretical brilliance, managerial skill and sheer energy as indispensable to the revolution, and rejected as inconceivable any idea of treachery on the part of his valued colleague. As the revolution progressed, though, and the party became increasingly alienated from the mass of the population, Coard's influence within the party grew.[41]

Bishop's loyalty to Marxist principles led him to sacrifice all the advantages in any potential power struggle with Coard. First, by accepting the idea of a "vanguard" party, drawing its mandate from Marxist theory rather than popular support, Bishop cut himself off from his source of strength—the people. The "vanguard" concept focused power in the party apparatus, where Coard had his strength. Second, by siding with Coard and the Bureau elite against the "left opportunism" of men like the Budhlalls and Stran Phillip, Bishop acquiesced in the elimination of many of his most loyal allies within the party. By 1980 Bishop had become—albeit unwittingly as yet—a prisoner of the conspiracy to make Grenada a communist state. It was a conspiracy he had willingly joined, but was temperamentally unsuited to consummate. When the logic of the PRG's policies began to create conditions that demanded "discipline" and "ruthlessness," to overcome the overwhelming resistance of the population, Bernard Coard became the man of the hour.

From the beginning the party had difficulty recruiting capable, trustworthy people to manage its ambitious social and economic programs. By 1981–82, NJM members found themselves overburdened with party offices, state positions, committees and other responsibilities. Details began to slip through the cracks, and the combination of too much work, too little organization, and too few successes were about to become overwhelming. The Coards and their supporters attributed the problems to "ill discipline," "poor organization," and "failure to ensure that meetings of the C.C. are conducted in accordance with Leninist principles; e.g. tight and firm chairmanship." The problem, in other words, was one of leadership.[42] The breach was about to open.

LENINIST PRINCIPLE

In October 1982, Bernard Coard suddenly resigned from the Central Committee. Refusing even to tender his resignation in person, he let Selwyn Strachan present his reasons. According to Strachan, Coard had been planning to resign for at least six months, but his decision had been hastened by recent incidents in which Bishop appeared to be undermining Coard's authority as chairman of the Organizing Committee. His basic reason for resigning, however, was overwork. Other party comrades were leaning on him too much to carry the burden of party work. Because he had to make the tough decisions, Coard felt he had acquired an image as a "hatchetman," and had become an objective "fetter" to the development of others. If the party were to progress, all must strive to attain higher standards of discipline in their own work, and Coard's resignation would force them to do so.[43]

Coard, Strachan explained, disagreed profoundly with the way the Central Committee was being run. He had analyzed the situation and saw three theoretical options: (1) he could resign; (2) he could remain and tolerate the current slackness in the Political Bureau and Central Committee; or (3) the party could resolve to introduce "Leninist measures" to reform itself. That would include replacing Bishop as chairman of the Central Committee and Political Bureau, chopping "dead weight" from the Central Committee, putting all Central Committee members into work committees, and expanding the Political Bureau. But if Coard remained on the Central Committee while proposing such reforms, it would be seen as a personal confrontation between himself and Bishop rather than as a matter of principle. So, Strachan explained, Coard felt his only real option was to resign.

Coard seemed to leave the door open just a crack for the

possibility of his return, provided that the party would, in his absence, implement the "Leninist measures" he proposed, particularly the removal of Bishop. The first reaction of Central Committee members, however, was indignation at Coard's arrogance in refusing to appear. The leaders debated forcing him to appear and considered disciplinary measures, including expulsion from the party. His wife, Phyllis, still a member of the CC, responded that Bernard believed the survival of the revolution was more important than his own membership. The real question, she continued, was whether the Central Committee believed there were indeed problems in the party, and whether Bernard's resignation was to be seen as a symptom of these.

At this cue, Coard's supporters went into action. Leon "Bogo" Cornwall agreed that Coard's resignation was not the main issue. The main issue was the fundamental problems facing the party. Ewart "Headache" Layne chimed in that Bernard's resignation was really a symptom of the main problems: slack organization, lack of discipline and the lax work habits of the party leadership. The party, Layne summarized, was at a crossroads; it could choose either of two paths. Making Coard's resignation the issue would be the easy petit bourgeois route: the party could pretend it was merely a leadership struggle, reprimand Coard, and paper over the real problems. This course, however, would lead to the NJM's deterioration into a social-democratic party, and the "degeneration of the revolution." The other option was "the Communist route—the road of Leninist standards and functioning." This would mean taking a hard look at individual and collective weaknesses and correcting them.

Cornwall, "Chaulky" Ventour and Liam "Owusu" James agreed with this analysis. The meeting then focused on Bishop's shortcomings as a leader. Strachan observed that Bishop was not yet a true Leninist leader: his lack of ideological study led him to make judgments based on pragmatic considerations instead of correct theoretical analysis. Phyllis added that she had been "shocked" by the "right-opportunist course" the party had been following under Bishop's leadership during 1982, including its shameful self-congratulation at having handled the "Gang of 26" threat firmly, when it had not acted firmly at all. Hudson Austin felt that discipline was essential: "I have criticized Maurice for softness; I hope his hand will now become a Marxist-Leninist-Stalinist hand."

Bishop may have been having doubts himself. He accepted most of the criticism, commending Layne for his analyses. He agreed he had not been fulfilling his role as leader. He had trouble setting priorities, he was undisciplined, and he did not take sufficient time for serious reflection. Could he change his style? He wasn't sure. He had been overtired and under psychological strain; personal problems had weighed on him since 1979. Moreover, there was the problem of his relationship with Coard. Maurice and Bernard had a personal and professional relationship that went back to their school days. But they had taken different approaches on many issues—the *Torchlight*, consultations with the USSR, decisions regarding various PRG programs—and Bernard's style was more aggressive. "Who is the real fetter," Bishop asked, "Bernard or me?"

Bishop's supporters were more forceful in his defense, and counterattacked. Whiteman, Radix, and Caldwell Taylor insisted that Coard should be present, and returned to the question of disciplinary action. Radix, long an opponent of Coard, went further. He charged that a "lack of frankness" in the party over the last 12 months had led to factionalism. Certain comrades—Radix made clear he was referring to Coard and his followers—were meeting in small groups to consult about their criticisms instead of going directly to the comrade concerned. Why, for example, had Coard's letter of resignation taken two weeks to reach the Central Committee? This was proof of the factionalism he spoke of.

Radix's sallies had no effect. Coard's supporters were far more adept at the criticism-self criticism game, and they went right back on the attack. Radix's position was especially vulnerable, since it was generally recognized that his own performance of duty had been substandard. Cornwall accused him of "general deterioration at all levels," and especially a petit-bourgeois attitude toward discipline and criticism. Others worried about his low ideological level, arrogance, and "bluntness." Then Layne announced that Radix's remarks about factionalism revealed petit-bourgeois opportunism; he must therefore be purged from the Political Bureau and perhaps even from the Central Committee.

Radix fell for it. Breaking the rules of the self-criticism game, he answered angrily that he had been unable to work up to standard at his state job because of illness (he had diabetes and some trouble with drinking), and that Coard's Organizing Committee had failed to assign him any party work, despite his asking. Criticisms levelled at him were dishonest, unprincipled, and opportunistic. He concluded angrily but ineffectually by saying there were "forces operating in the party which cause me some concern, as all issues have not been brought out."

This outburst sealed Radix's fate. Cornwall, Ventour, Layne and Phyllis Coard led the others in concluding that Radix's violent rejection of criticism had been "uncomradely," and confirmed that he lacked the Marxist-Leninist qualities for Political Bureau and Central Committee membership. Radix lost his composure completely, protested once more that the "Bolshevik" style of self criticism introduced was "too draconian," then suddenly resigned from the PRG and the party. With a parting warning that "right opportunism has been smashed but left opportunism must also be looked for," Radix wished the party and its leaders every success, and tearfully pledged to help as much as he could in a private capacity.

Caldwell Taylor, Kamau McBarnette, Fitzroy Bain and Unison Whiteman were also found wanting. Phyllis Coard called Taylor's performance "borderline," and pointed to his failure to prevent the collapse of party work in St. Andrew's. Cornwall accused him of poor judgment, and referred to some "frightening" mystical-sounding remarks Taylor had made about people having an "aura." His ideological development was found to be excessively low, and he was removed from the Central Committee. Whiteman was criticized for poor performance as agriculture minister, "softness," "political timidity," and his weak grasp of Marxism-Leninism. The Committee agreed he was to be "severely warned." Taylor and Whiteman were assigned, along with Hudson Austin, Fitzroy Bain, and Ian Bartholemew, to attend an eight-week crash course in Marxism-Leninism to be taught by Bernard Coard, using texts by Joseph Stalin.

Bishop was also reprimanded, albeit more carefully. He received high marks on most aspects of his work, but was nevertheless criticized by Strachan and Cornwall for his general slackness and for analytical weakness in applying Marxist theory. "Owusu" James commended Bishop's overall leadership qualities but noted, with Phyllis's concurrence, that his major weaknesses were "softness" and "too much humanitarianism."

Bishop, who always obliged himself to play these Marxist sports by the rules, accepted their criticisms. At Phyllis's suggestion, he was removed from supervising militia work and put in charge of overseeing rural workers, and a personal assistant "of high political reliability" was to be found for him. The Central Committee also agreed to introduce standards for "Leninist chairmanship," to create a Disciplinary Committee, and to draw up a Code of Conduct and Discipline and a party constitution. Finally, in line with Coard's suggestion to expand the Political Bureau, comrades Layne, James, and Ventour, all Coard allies, were immediately appointed to that body, and Phyllis Coard was to be assessed for possible appointment at a later date.

It was a complete victory for Coard. Through his supporters in the Central Committee he had turned the debate over his own resignation into a referendum on Bishop's leadership. The three Bishop supporters who had ventured to press for disciplinary action against Coard had instead been disciplined themselves, and others close to Bishop were criticized for their unsatisfactory performance. Although Bishop was not himself removed, he would hereafter be surrounded by Coard's staunchest allies, not only in the Central Committee, but in the Political Bureau as well. Through them, Coard could continue to influence policy while avoiding any personal responsibility for the mounting difficulties confronting the party in the months ahead. When conditions once again reached a crisis, there would be only one man at the top to blame—and only one alternative to replace him.

The next major self-assessment of the NJM leadership was planned for March 1983, but was postponed because of the "invasion threat" that month. A six-and-a-half-day marathon meeting was finally held from July 13–19, billed as "the first full-scale wholistic plenary of the C.C." The findings were grim and the assessment grimly ideological. The main feature of the present political and economic situation was determined to be the "continued failure of the party to transform itself ideologically and organizationally and to exercise firm leadership along a Leninist path."

The work of the mass organizations had "stagnated" and political work in the various regions of the island had been "weak and ineffective." Anti-communism and the ideological offensive of the church had been gaining ground. A cash-flow crisis in the economy had slowed or halted capital improvement projects, caused layoffs, and shaken the confidence of the masses. Worst of all, there had been "the emergence of deep petty-bourgeois manifestations and influence in the Party" which had led to "two ideological trends." Yet there was a ray of hope: The Central Committee concluded that the work of the C.C. and Political Bureau had improved marginally in the period under review."[44]

Even this faint note of optimism was short-lived. Critics of Bishop's leadership called for another emergency Central Committee meeting on August 26. At that meeting Bishop's critics claimed that little progress had been made on reforms agreed upon in July, that party members were dissatisfied with the level of guidance from the top, and that, in sum, "We are seeing the beginning of the disintegration of the party." To address these problems, they demanded that all CC members assigned abroad be recalled for another special plenary meeting.[45]

The Coard faction had decided to take off the gloves. When the special plenary convened on September 14, "Headache" Layne reviewed the appalling state of affairs in every area of the party's work and announced that the revolution faced its greatest danger since 1979. The party, he said, had begun to crumble; it lacked a political line and was deviating into "right opportunism." The fault lay squarely with the Central Committee. Ventour and Cornwall seconded this, adding examples of their own. Phyllis Coard scorned the dishonesty of the CC's July claim of an "improvement in work," and predicted that if the current situation continued, the party would "disintegrate within 3–6 months." All agreed that the situation was critical.

Finally James came to the point. The main fetter in the Central Committee, he declared, "is the quality of leadership of the party and the CC, and in particular the leadership of Maurice Bishop." Bishop had tremendous strengths, but he was weak in the areas that now were needed most: Leninist organization and discipline, depth of ideological clarity, and brilliance in strategy and tactics. (It is revealing of the Coard faction's attitudes that, with their country on the verge of economic, social, and political collapse, they regarded "ideological clarity" and "Leninist organization" as the indispensable qualities of leadership.) Cornwall, Layne, and Ventour immediately concurred, and others admitted they accepted James's analysis. George Louison, one of the CC's most respected members, agreed that Bishop's leadership was the party's "number one weakness," but saw a problem: Bishop was still the best leader the NJM had.

James was prepared with a solution. Bishop and Coard should share the leadership, he said, with Bishop focusing on relations with the masses and Coard taking charge of the party organization. Coard would chair the Organizing Committee and the weekly Political Bureau meetings, while Bishop would preside over monthly sessions of the Central Committee. Louison dismissed this contrivance. Coard's return to senior party posts would be welcome, he said, and if leaders were convinced Bishop could not improve, then he would have to be removed. Joint leadership was not workable. Despite an overwhelming majority in favor of joint leadership, Louison voted against the measure, and Unison Whiteman abstained.[46]

Deprived of a clear-cut victory in the Central Committee, Coard's faction prepared to take its case to a general meeting of all full party members on Sunday, September 25. Louison had left the country on the 17th as head of the advance team for Bishop's forthcoming trip to Eastern Europe. Bishop himself, stung by the personal attack against him, had asked for some time alone to consider his response, and promised to return on September 24. In his absence, Bernard Coard returned to chair the Central Committee, which continued meeting from September 19 to 23, and began putting in place the reforms he intended for the party.[47] But when the membership convened on the 25th

Coard refused to come. He explained in a note that it would not be fitting for him to attend if Bishop were not also present.

Instead, "Owusu" James led the attack. Speaking to all the party members, James reviewed the charges made in the CC: the party was disintegrating, and Bishop's leadership was chiefly to blame. He presented the Central Committee's "decision" to establish a joint leadership "marrying together the strengths of Comrades Maurice Bishop and Bernard Coard," commenting that this model only acknowledged a reality that had existed in the party for the last 10 years. The Coard faction also distributed a report (falsely represented as the record of the August 26 emergency meeting) summarizing its arguments, exposing an alleged coverup of Coard's 1982 resignation, and charging that the CC had followed a "right opportunist" course since then by failing to address the root causes of Coard's correct action. Layne remarked that Bishop's reaction to criticism in the Central Committee had been "petty bourgeois." He added that he had spoken to all CC members who supported the "majority position," and that all had agreed to resign if the "road of opportunism" were chosen at this meeting. Strachan supported this, noting that in failing to accede to the wishes of the CC majority, Bishop showed contempt for the CC and for the principle of democratic centralism.[48]

At this point, the meeting voted to send for Bishop and Coard. Bishop was asked to explain remarks he had allegedly made about being dissatisfied with the CC report. Realizing he was outnumbered, Bishop answered carefully. The concept of joint leadership did not bother him, he said, but some aspects of it required mature reflection. Some comrades evidently had reservations about his leadership which they had not raised openly at the July plenary. He was concerned about the real meaning of the CC's position: if he lacked the qualities to be leader, then the "joint leadership" idea was an unprincipled compromise, for it would be wrong for him to represent the party to the masses while lacking the confidence of the Central Committee. He was considering instead the option of withdrawing from the leadership entirely, but had not yet made up his mind. It was up to the CC to go ahead and clarify its own position in the meantime.[49]

Layne immediately pounced on Bishop's reference to dishonest criticism. Bishop's implication that there was "a conspiracy to remove him but at this time for tactical reasons we are going half way" showed "gross contempt for the intelligence of the CC." One or two others, though, were not so sure. Unison Whiteman expressed his own theoretical and practical doubts about the joint leadership idea, suggesting that if Bishop lacked the qualities to lead by himself, "collective leadership and not joint leadership solves the problem." Fitzroy Bain observed that there had been some private "caucusing" in the CC, and if this reflected a plot, it must be crushed. He also noted that George Louison was not present, although he had strong feelings on the joint leadership question.

On the whole, the party rank-and-file were alarmed at the state of the party and supported the Central Committee "majority position." Further harsh words about Bishop's "petty bourgeois behavior" gave way gradually to exhortations from the floor that he accept the criticisms in a comradely way. One member rose to say that this was "the most glorious day in the life of the party because of the frankness and honesty with which the vast majority of Comrades are carrying on the discussion." Others seconded these thoughts, adding that this historic meeting proved the party was developing and maturing along a Marxist-Leninist path.[50]

Bishop was evidently moved. When the members called on the two leaders to speak, Coard rose to capture the mounting tide of euphoria. This was indeed a historic meeting, he affirmed, since every CC member had come forth with clear and reasoned positions, showing the way forward to a genuine Marxist-Leninist party. The general membership, too, had spoken thoughtfully and with sincere commitment. Vowing his deep confidence in the future building of communism, Coard pledged to devote every ounce of effort to this process, as he knew Bishop would do as well. Bishop, caught up in the spirit of the moment, rose, embraced Coard, and announced "I accept the criticism and will fulfill the decision in practice." Joint leadership, he said, would help push the party and the revolution forward. The meeting ended with a stirring chorus of the Internationale and embraces all around.[51]

The next day Bishop left for Hungary and Czechoslovakia,

where he met Louison. When Louison heard the news of Bishop's capitulation, he was horrified. Louison argued forcefully that Bishop's first instinct had been right—that "joint leadership" was simply a front for Coard's power grab, and that Bishop would soon be rendered powerless unless he fought back immediately. Bishop was convinced, and resolved to take Louison's advice. On the way back to Grenada the party made an unscheduled stop in Cuba where Bishop met Castro. But Bishop did not raise the subject of the power struggle. Characteristically, he was determined to work out the party's problems within the Central Committee, avoiding any outward appearance of disunity. But when the CC leaders received a phone call from Havana apprising them of Bishop's change of heart and of the unscheduled stop in Cuba, they imagined the worst.[52]

LENINIST DISCIPLINE

The Coard group had already taken steps to secure control of the army by moving Cornwall and Layne into high-ranking military posts. Austin, the army commander, was also with them. Now, to solidify support among the troops, Coard and his colleagues suddenly announced that, in the spirit of the new, reorganized party, the CC had decided to award soldiers an allowance of $30.00 a month for each dependent. They also stepped up "political education" work in the armed forces.[53]

When Bishop and his party arrived at Pearls Airport on October 8 they were met, not by the usual Central Committee delegation, but by Selwyn Strachan in a T-shirt. The atmosphere was tense, and grew more tense over the following days as mutual suspicions thickened. Coard made no attempt to contact Bishop, nor did any of the other CC members except Hudson Austin. Coard and his lieutenants held mysterious meetings at Mt. Weldale, not far from the Prime Minister's residence. Rumors circulated within the NJM that party leaders were not sleeping in their houses, that Bishop was trying to establish one-man rule, and that an "Afghanistan solution" was being considered—i.e., liquidating Bishop and replacing him with a more orthodox communist. Nazim Burke and a few other middle-ranking party members sent a letter begging Bishop for an urgent meeting to discuss the situation in the party.[54]

On Wednesday, October 12, the storm broke. A Political Bureau meeting was scheduled for that day, at which Bishop intended to demand an explanation for his CC colleagues' behavior toward him and to review his misgivings about the practicability of joint leadership.

The Coard group was anticipating a power play, and took steps to prepare for it. Shortly after midnight, security chief Keith Roberts summoned a meeting of the Prime Minister's security detail and informed them that the protection of Bishop's life was no longer their primary responsibility. At 7:00 a.m., Coard's supporters in the People's Revolutionary Army held a secret meeting and passed a resolution declaring their loyalty to the Central Committee and its decisions, supporting the idea of joint leadership, and calling for expulsion from the party of "all elements who do not submit to, uphold, and implement in practice the decision of the Central Committee."[55]

Meanwhile, Bishop had begun to take his own precautions. Apparently getting word of the Coard group's activities, at 7:30 Wednesday morning he summoned his personal bodyguards, Cletus St. Paul and Errol George. He explained that he believed Bernard and Phyllis Coard were planning to kill him. He asked them to help him draw up lists of trustworthy people who could be contacted to get the word out. Some of the names mentioned were Richard Hart, Ashley Taylor and Jimmy Emmanuel. Jacqueline Creft had her own list of names to check, beginning with Bishop's mother, Alimenta Bishop. Mrs. Bishop later recalled that Creft suddenly appeared at her home looking grave and said, "I don't know how to tell you this, but today is the day they plan to take Maurice up to the fort for a meeting and kill him, and blame it on the CIA." Creft told her to start calling her friends and letting them know, which she did.[56]

The Political Bureau convened at 9:00 a.m. to discuss the PRA resolution and George Louison's transgressions. That meeting, however, was inconclusive; the real confrontation came at the Central Committee meeting that afternoon. As usual on such occasions, Bernard Coard was absent, pleading illness. Instead, Strachan, Cornwall, Ventour, Ian St. Bernard, and Phyllis took the lead. Their first priority was to dispose of Louison, placing primary blame on him for "manipulating" Bishop and lying to party members in Hungary about the September 25 Central Committee decision. They also mentioned the rumors, now rife throughout the island, that the Coards were planning to murder Bishop and stage a coup. "Owusu" James revealed that Errol George had made a full confession and that Cletus St. Paul was about to be taken into custody. James also charged that St. Paul had tried (presumably on Bishop's behalf) to have Coard assassinated a year ago after his 1982 resignation, and had been predicting during and after the recent East European trip that "blood will flow." He also charged Louison with spreading rumors of a coming coup.[57]

Bishop and Louison counterattacked. On whose authority had a PRA meeting been called that morning without notifying him or Austin, Bishop demanded, and who was the author of the PRA resolution? Who had originated rumors within the party that he was guilty of "cultism," "egoism," and "one-manism," or claiming that he "cannot go beyond social democracy?" Why were comrades who reported to him being called "counter-revolutionaries"? Louison admitted to addressing party members in Hungary but denied any conspiracy, observing that those now holding private caucuses and security meetings at all hours of the night were not being accused of anti-party activity. When James proposed to arrest St. Paul, Fitzroy Bain shot back that those responsible for discussing Bishop's life at 1:00 that morning should be arrested, too. He threatened: "I will march 3,000 people here tonight." Louison suggested arresting as well those people who were spreading the "Afghanistan" line. At that point Ventour pulled his gun. Bain said he was going to vomit, protesting that some comrades apparently had no right to speak and that there was "too much Marxist-Leninist jargon involved; too much one-sidedness."[58]

The Central Committee proceeded with the business at hand. On a motion by "Headache" Layne, members voted one after another to expel Louison from the Political Bureau and the Central Committee. Bain warned, "we are going to end up with a revolution without the people."

The meeting then turned its attention to Bishop: Strachan informed him that he would have seven days to take an unambiguous position "on which you are willing to *act*"; and that his decision would determine whether or not he would remain in the party. The communist parties of Cuba and the Soviet Union would be advised of the situation. As the meeting was drawing to a close, James suddenly came in with the news that a few people had mobilized a section of the St. Paul's militia, seized arms, and were headed for Mt. Weldale to protect Bishop from the Coards. The CC members insisted that Bishop go on the radio to deny the assassination rumor. Cornwall warned Bain against any attempt to follow up on his threat to mobilize workers. The excitable Bain broke down and cried.[59]

At midnight, Bishop went on the air and denounced the rumor about the Coards. The party was firm and united, he said, and security forces were vigorously investigating the source of the lie. (The last part was true—Hudson Austin had taken some soldiers up to Bishop's mother's house and demanded to know who told her the assassination story, but she indicated it reached her through the grapevine.)

Meanwhile the Coard group, shaken by the militia revolt, was taking steps to remove all militia weapons from St. Paul's and St. David's (where there had also been trouble), reinforce PRA units in St. Patrick's, and strengthen forces at Fort Rupert. The armed forces were put on alert, and Bishop's house was quietly put under surveillance. Coard and his colleagues also worked feverishly to carry their version of the day's confrontation to the party in preparation for an emergency meeting of the general membership the next day, October 13. Bishop was not informed of the meeting and only heard of it that afternoon, when Vince Noel, who had been speaking to Ventour, came by to ask him about the "madness" going on in the party. Noel begged him to set the record straight at the meeting Ventour had said would take place later that day.[60]

When Bishop arrived, he found the stage set and the script well rehearsed for the ritual of his disgrace and removal from power. With Coard presiding, Selwyn Strachan gave a long presentation, interrupted by frequent applause, reviewing the CC's actions of the previous day. "Can we allow one man to hold up the party?" he asked the assembled membership. "No!" came the reply. "Can we allow a minority to hold the party to ransom?" "No!" The PRA resolution was read, and "Owusu" James detailed the history of the assassination rumor, producing a photocopy of Errol George's confession. He then announced several security measures, supposedly to protect the lives of CC members: Bishop was to be confined in his house indefinitely, disarmed and with his phones cut off; Major Einstein Louison (who had been caught spreading Bishop's version of recent events among the troops) was to be suspended and placed under house arrest; and the people found spreading the infamous rumor were being called in for a warning, or detained.

When Bishop got his chance to speak he started on the defensive. He confessed having "petty bourgeois weaknesses." He claimed he had never had problems with joint leadership in principle, and vehemently denied spreading the rumor. Louison and Bain also tried to defend themselves. But the Coard group resumed the attack, backed by rank-and-file members horrified at the "contemptuous" attitude of Bishop and the others toward the CC majority decisions. "Headache" Layne finally demanded Bishop's expulsion from the party, adding that "the only question, then, is whether he be allowed to operate as a private citizen or arrested and court martialed" for stirring up counter-revolution.[61]

Layne's motion was never acted upon; the Coard group had already won. Bishop was escorted back to his home under arrest, and was joined there voluntarily by his lover, Jackie Creft. Both camps began jockeying for position in the inevitable final show-down. At first, Coard appeared to have everything sewn up. The army was under control, the security services were hunting for potential pro-Bishop agitators, and the NJM cadre, inspired by the October 13 morality play, began visiting mass organizations and workplaces the following day to explain the official Central Committee line.

But it was soon clear that the masses were not taking the news very well. On October 14, Selwyn Strachan announced to a crowd in downtown St. George's that Coard had replaced Bishop as Prime Minister. The crowd chased Strachan off the street. Later Coard issued a press release stating that he had resigned from the government in order to dispel false rumors that he had plotted to kill Bishop. The Coards and Strachan thereupon dropped from public view.[62]

On October 15, Radix and Bain led a street demonstration demanding the release and reinstatement of Bishop. Keith Roberts's security agents reported popular grumbling about wanting to hear Bishop's side of the story, accusations that Strachan and others were slandering the Prime Minister, and slogans of "no Bishop, no Coard, no work, no school." One agent recommended "comrades should avoid slandering Maurice—deal with the main issue." Fitzroy Bain was stirring up the agricultural workers; employees in some shops and industries were restive and discussing strikes; and the government ministries were grinding to a halt.

The Cubans, too, were a matter of concern. When briefed on October 13 about the CC actions, Ambassador Rizo, a good friend of Bishop, was shocked and deeply upset. He had been taken completely unawares. Castro was equally horrified. On October 15, he fired off a letter to the NJM Central Committee calling charges that Bishop had briefed him on internal NJM problems "a miserable piece of slander." Everything that had recently happened in Grenada was "distasteful" to the Cuban comrades, Castro continued, and there was great respect and sympathy in his country for Comrade Bishop. "Even explaining the events to our people will not be easy."[63]

On October 15, Bernard Coard tried to negotiate with Louison and the party dissidents. Coard tried to persuade them that joint leadership was ideologically correct and workable. But Louison responded that the Central Committee's actions were destroying the party and had created the prospect of civil war; Maurice must be released. The masses could not be held back indefinitely. Coard countered that he could wait out the masses, allowing them to wear themselves out demonstrating until they were ready to go back to peace and quiet, as Gairy had done in 1973–74. After much wrangling, Coard promised on October 17 to seek a concrete proposal from the Central Committee.

But by October 18, Louison and his colleagues grew tired of waiting. Deciding that Coard was just stalling for time, Louison, Whiteman, Housing Minister Norris Bain and Lyden Ramdhanny formally resigned from the government, and began organizing demonstrations. That day saw massive street protests in St. George's and a student demonstration in Grenville that briefly shut down Pearls Airport. Keith Roberts's spies reported that the Cubans at the international airport construction site were "inciting the local workers to go and get their Prime Minister." By nightfall, Louison and Radix had been jailed, and Ramdhanny warned to stay at home.[64]

That night, a CC delegation of Austin, Layne, James, and Ian Bartholemew went to the Prime Minister's residence with a final proposal for a compromise: Bishop would be removed from the CC and from his position as Commander in Chief of the army, but would remain Prime Minister and a regular party member. A negotiating team would be appointed to mend the rift in the party, and Bishop would announce this fact publicly. Finally, Bishop would accept full responsibility for the assassination rumor. Bishop agreed to consider all the proposals except the last and to have an answer by morning. First, though, he wanted to talk to Louison, Whiteman, and Rizo.[65]

Louison, still under arrest, was accordingly brought to Bishop's residence the following morning, October 19, at about 9:00, and the two had breakfast together. Whiteman, however, was down in St. George's with Fitzroy and Norris Bain, whipping up a mob of some 10,000 people. People were streaming in from all over the country—not only Bishop supporters, but apolitical farmers and workers, students, Gairyites, and people of every other description, united by their sympathy for their captive Prime Minister, and even more by their loathing of Coard and all he stood for. Lyden Ramdhanny was back in Grenville organizing buses and trucks to carry more people in from the parishes. While the bulk of the crowd remained down in the market square, milling and chanting, waiting for Bishop to come and speak, Whiteman led a couple of thousand people up to Bishop's home in the hills above. Ignoring the PRA guards who fired warning shots into the air, the crowd swept in through a rear entrance and emerged with Bishop. A few minutes later, Brother Leonard answered a rap at the door of Presentation College, whose students had long since poured out of their classrooms onto the streets. He was greeted by an 11-year-old former student who announced with beaming pride, "We have him. We have our Prime Minister."[66]

Bishop was in terrible shape, badly worn down by days of constant stress and little sleep. Later reports suggested he had not been eating, for fear of being poisoned. He seemed temporarily confused as the crowd bore him along triumphantly to the vehicles waiting outside, choosing first to lead the crowd on foot, then climbing into a car, then a truck, then finally another car. Whether because of his weakness or for security reasons, it was decided not to continue the procession all the way down Market Hill to the square, but instead to swing left on Church Street and head for Fort Rupert. As the crowd surged past St. George's Anglican Church, Archdeacon Huggins waved from the front lawn of the rectory. They wound down to the intersection at Young Street, then up the steep hill past the St. James Hotel and the Presbyterian Church to the massive 18th-century fortress on a bluff overlooking the city.[67]

They arrived at about 11:00. Bishop and his lieutenants set up headquarters in an administrative building outside the walls and demanded that the garrison lay down its arms. The officers complied, Major Chris Stroude locking the weapons in the armory and presenting the keys to Bishop. Refreshments were ordered up for the crowd. Bishop, still shaky and being attended by nurses from the nearby hospital, dispatched his press spokesman Don Rojas to the telephone exchange down in the city to arrange a hookup that would allow him to address the crowd in the market square over a public address system. Rojas was also to try to contact overseas news media to get Bishop's side of the story out to the world. The crowd at the Fort continued to swell; people began shouting for guns, but Bishop refused to arm them. At about 12:15, a repairman managed to get the phones working. A few minutes later, though, people in the crowd outside noticed some army trucks winding down the hill from the direction of Fort Frederick. Some, sensing trouble, began to disperse.

Bishop and his followers had never really believed that the PRA would turn its guns on the people, and the soldiers' unwillingness to fire on the crowd that rescued Bishop from his house appeared to confirm that judgement. Once the soldiers at Fort Rupert had surrendered peacefully, there seemed little reason to doubt that the army would bow to the will of the people. Once again, Bishop had underestimated his adversary. Convinced they were now in a fight to the finish, Coard and his supporters had selected a handful of fiercely loyal junior officers to man the three armored personnel carriers that now came roaring down on Fort Rupert, backed up by a truckload of elite PRA troops. The convoy paused a moment for the traffic control point on Young Street, then barged across the intersection, mashing up a car on the way, and up the hill toward the Fort. It stopped again briefly next to the St. James Hotel to scout out potential resistance ahead, then, finding the way clear, surged forward into the crowd with guns blazing.

Inside Bishop's makeshift headquarters there were two heavy explosions as rocket grenades pounded into the building. Fragments of the room flew everywhere. Then came several minutes of heavy machine gun fire. The crowd ran screaming in all directions, some hurling themselves over the steep walls of the Fort. Finally, one of the officers of the garrison screamed for the attacking troops to cease firing. The shooting stopped, and a voice from outside ordered the people in the building to come out with their hands up. As they filed out past the crumpled bodies of men, women, and children mowed down in the attack, Bishop, Whiteman, the two Bains, and several others were pulled out of the crowd and lined up against a wall in the interior courtyard of the Fort. There, under a faded slogan reading "TOWARDS HIGHER DISCIPLINE IN THE PRA," they were methodically gunned down by officers of the People's Revolutionary Army. Watching from a cell at Richmond Hill prison on the heights above, Louison and Radix saw a white flare rise from Fort Rupert—a signal, they later learned, to the Central Committee at Fort Frederick, indicating that its orders had been carried out.

NOTES

1. Letter from Fr. Cyril Lamontagne to Maurice Bishop, dated November 9, 1979 (GD 104714); letter from Eileen Byer, Secretary of the CCG, to the Prime Minister, dated November 14, 1979 (GD 104714); numerous letters written to Maurice Bishop in November–December 1979 by Grenadian citizens (GD unnumbered).

2. "Report of the Delegation Sent to Grenada by the America Department with the Aim of Starting the Gathering of Sources for the Characterization of the Religious Situation in the Country, and the Contacts for Further Cooperation between the *PCC* and the NJM Regarding the Question," dated August 13–24, 1982 and submitted October 14, 1982 by Aurelio Alonso Tejada (GD unnumbered), p.10; conversations with Bishop Charles, Archdeacon Huggins, and other Grenadians.

3. Untitled report, dated 18.30 hrs., February 11, 1980 and labelled "TOP SECRET" (GD unnumbered); Maurice Bishop, "A Permanent, Standing Commitment to Freedom of Worship and Religion," speech delivered over Radio Free Grenada, February 15, 1980, in Marcus and Taber, *Maurice Bishop Speaks*, p. 66; conversations with Archdeacon Huggins and others.

4. "The Dominican Letter," *Grenada Newsletter*, February 23, 1980, p. 5; conversation with Alister Hughes.

5. Bishop, "A Permanent, Standing Commitment," pp. 60–69.

6. *Ibid.*, *Grenada Newsletter*, February 23, 1980, p. 5; conversation with Alister Hughes.

7. *Grenada Newsletter*, February 23, 1980, pp. 7, 15, 16; *Ibid.*, May 10, 1980, pp. 1–5, 7; conversations with Alister Hughes, Lyden Ramdhanny, Percival Campbell (Manager of River Antoine Estate), Kennedy Budhlall, and others. River Antoine was eventually seized by the PRG under the land reform law, but was returned to the De Gales after the fall of the PRG.

8. *Grenada Newsletter*, May 10, 1980, pp. 1, 5; "The Truth of the Revolution," tract circulated by Stran Phillip, undated, probably issued about the first quarter of 1980 (GD 104884).

9. Conversation with Kennedy Budhlall.

10. *Grenada Newsletter*, June 21, 1980, pp. 1, 5, 7; *Ibid.*, June 28, 1980, p. 1; *Ibid.*, August 16, 1980, pp. 4, 6; *Ibid.*, September 20, 1980, pp. 2–3; *Ibid.*, October 4, 1980, p. 3; *Ibid.*, November 15, 1980, pp. 1, 9, 18; *Ibid.*, November 29, 1980, pp. 1, 4; "Human Right Tribune: The Grenada Situation," crude, undated leaflet

attacking the NJM, the "Socialist Fascist K.G.B.," Cubans, etc. (GD 001990); "Inside the Grenada Horror Movie — 'Nightmare in Grenada,' Brought to You by the Committee of Grenada Freedom Fighters Against Tyranny in Grenada," well-written six-page tract, also undated, apparently printed professionally by emigre dissidents about early 1981 (GD 105440); Sunshine, *Peaceful Rev.*, p. 68; conversations with Alister Hughes, Cecil Horsford (former Inspector, Criminal Investigations Division, Grenada Police Service), and others.

11. "People's Law No. 46 of 1980: A Law to Create Offences Relating to Terrorism, to Provide for the mode of Trial and for Connected Purposes," dated September 29, 1980, in *Grenada: The People's Laws 1980* (St. George's: Government Printing Office, 1981), pp. 373–384; "Prime Minister Bishop's Address to the Nation in October, 1980 (GD 003160); "Plan of C.I. Operations," undated document setting forth procedures for surveillance of various regions and social groups, and protection of security risks (GD 100738); memo from Head Special Branch (Michael Roberts) to Minister of National Security (Bishop) on "Unrest at St. Patrick's/St. Andrew's Area," reporting on alleged subversive activities and suspicious meetings among farmers and others, dated January 23, 1981 (GD 002890); memo from Head Special Branch to Minister of National Security on "Statements of Tony Buxo (owner of Grenadian Optical Laboratories)," dated July 2, 1981 (GD 103523); intelligence reports on "Counter Revolutionary Activities" of various individuals, dated July 15, 1981 (GD unnumbered); memo from O. C. C. Linton to Captain H. Romain, "Situation Report" on River Road area of St. George's, providing information on activities of various organizations and social groups (GD 102607); letter (in Spanish), dated May 5, 1983, from Ramiro Valdes Menendez, Cuban Minister of the Interior, to "Lian" (actually Liam) James, NJM security chief, introducing Major Nelson Guerra Rodriguez as the new head of the Cuban mission to "the organization which you direct" (GD unnumbered).

12. *Grenada Newsletter*, August 10, 1980, p. 23; packet of handwritten statements on alleged beatings and torture by PRA officers, dated July 1980 (GD 105634).

13. "Bits of Information," Special Branch report, undated, on various items of security concern including the activities of a "reactionary group" in the Police Service (GD 104687); report from Acting Inspector Godfrey Augustine to the Commissioner of Police, dated

November 30, 1979, on "Prevention of Investigations by a Few Members of the People's Revolutionary Army—P.R.A.—into a Shooting Incident at Morne Rouge" (GD 104260); conversations with Luckey Bernard, Cecil Horsford, and others.

Luckey Bernard apparently was kept on in his senior position in the Police Service partly because Gairy's Mongoose Gang had tried to poison him just before the NJM coup. Bernard was recuperating in a hospital when the coup occurred. Although intensely religious and bitterly critical of the regime (he repeatedly sought encouragement from American Embassy personnel in his hope that the U.S. would intervene militarily against the PRG), he managed to maintain the impression with his superiors that he was politically reliable enough to be kept on. A Cuban report on him in 1982 recommended that "Attention and continuity should be given to him for combining the presence in the Church [as a lay minister] with a responsibility in the Administration, but he gives no indication of possibilities for progress in his positions" ("Report of . . . the America Department," Annex 2, p. 10). Bernard died in Texas in spring 1983 from the aftereffects of the 1979 poisoning.

14. Minutes of PB meeting, May 13, 1981 (GD 103448), p. 3; minutes of EB meeting, June 5, 1981 (GD unnumbered), p. 7; minutes of CC meeting June 6, 1981 (GD unnumbered), p. 8; minutes of CC meeting, June 10, 1981 (GD unnumbered), p. 2.

15. Minutes of EB meeting, June 12, 1981 (GD unnumbered), p. 3; conversations with Leslie Pierre, Alister Hughes, Lloyd Noel, and others.

16. Minutes of PB meeting, May 27, 1981 (GD 103448); minutes of CC extraordinary meetings, June 14–16, 1981 (GD unnumbered), pp. 1–2. The NFU, or National Farmers' Union, was a spontaneous organization of larger farmers, some of them excluded from membership in the PFU because of the extent of their holdings, who had banded together to promote their common interests. The NJM had been trying to penetrate the NFU to get a better idea of its membership and motives, but had had little success so far.

17. Minutes of CC extraordinary meetings, June 14–16, 1981, pp. 2–8.

18. Maurice Bishop, "Freedom of the Press and Imperialist Destabilization," in Marcus and Taber, *Maurice Bishop Speaks*, pp. 150–166.

19. Minutes of CC meeting, June 24, 1981 (GD 003340); minutes of PB meeting, June 24, 1981 (GD unnumbered); minutes of PB/EB meeting, June 26, 1981 (GD 103448); minutes of PB meetings,

June 27 and July 1, 1981 (GD unnumbered); minutes of EB meeting, July 10, 1981 (GD 003306); conversations with Alister Hughes and Leslie Pierre.

20. Minutes of CC meeting, September 30, 1981 (GD unnumbered), p. 1; minutes of CC meeting, December 30, 1981 (GD 104060), pp. 3–4.

21. Minutes of PB meeting, May 20, 1981 (GD unnumbered), p. 2.

22. *Ibid.*, pp. 2–4.

23. "Report of . . . the America Department," pp. 1, 15–17.

24. *Ibid.*, pp. 2, 5–7, 17–19.

25. "Analysis—The Church in Grenada," Top Secret report from Officer Cadet Michael Roberts to Major Keith Roberts, dated March 15, 1983 (GD unnumbered).

26. *Ibid.*, minutes of PB meeting, December 29, 1982 (GD 103448), p. 5; minutes of PB meeting, January 5, 1983 (GD 100276), p. 3.

27. "Analysis of the Church in Grenada," submitted by Major Keith Roberts, dated July 12, 1983 (GD unnumbered); Bishop notes of CC meeting, October 12, 1982 (GD unnumbered); minutes of PB/EB meeting, September 7, 1983 (GD 104451), p. 14.

28. Bishop notes of CC meeting, September 14, 1983 (GD unnumbered); conversation with Archdeacon Huggins.

29. "Analysis of O.C. [Organizing Committee]," dated March 28, 1983 (GD unnumbered); "C.I. Weekly Analysis/Report," dated April 6, 1983 (GD 103745); "Special Report to Security and Defence Committee and the Political Bureau," dated April 16, 1983 (GD 103745).

30. "List of Persons in Detention as from 1st January 1982" (GD 104947); Letter to "Comrade Minister of Legal Affairs" from the Preventive Detention Tribunal, undated (GD 002118); minutes of PB meeting, June 3, 1981 (GD 103448), p. 1.

31. Conversations with Archdeacon Huggins, Patricia White (Christian Science practitioner in Grenada who regularly visited detainees), and numerous former detainees.

32. Letter from the Trinidad and Tobago Bureau on Human Rights to Ian Jacobs in the Prime Minister's Office, Grenada, dated October 23, 1979 (GD 104262); draft of a letter to the Secretary, British Section, Amnesty International regarding "Detainees in Grenada," dated October 12, 1982 (GD unnumbered), conversation with a Red Cross representative in Grenada.

33. Letters from Maurice Bishop's files (GD unnumbered); conversations with numerous Grenadians.

34. Conversations with Beverley Steele, Winston Whyte, Oliver Raeburn, Luckey Bernard, and many other Grenadians both during and after the PRG period.

35. Conversations with a British media advisor, Grenadian media professionals, and numerous other Grenadians.

36. Conversations with Herbert Blaize and numerous Grenadians.

37. "St. Andrew's P.C.B. Report," dated June 29, 1983 (GD 103745); "Report on St. George's P.C.B. Work, Mid-March to End of June, 1983," submitted to a CC plenary meeting in July 1983 (GD 103745); "Report on West Coast P.C.B.—January–June 1983" (GD 103745); report to Political Bureau on "Present Situation of the Youth Work," submitted by Youth Committee (NYO), December 18, 1982 (GD 003085); "Report on Youth Work from January–June 1983," dated July 2, 1983 (GD 103745); minutes of OC meeting, October 11, 1982 (GD unnumbered), p. 1.

38. Bishop notes of CC meeting, September 14, 1983 (GD unnumbered); minutes of EC meeting, December 31, 1982 (GD 103470), p. 1; conversations with a Canadian technical advisor in Grenada and with numerous Grenadians.

39. "Workers Education Classes: Weekly Report No. 1 for Week: Fri. April 29–Fri. May 6th, 1983," dated May 8, 1983 (GD unnumbered); "Worker Education Classes Weekly Report No. 6 for Week June 13–17 [1983]" (GD unnumbered); "Worker Education Tutors Seminar—Friday 9.9.83–Saturday 10.9.83" (GD 003196).

40. William C. Adams, "Grenada Update," *Public Opinion*, February/ March 1984; conversation with Professor Adams, August 31, 1984.

41. Conversations with Lyden Ramdhanny, and with Mrs. Alimenta Bishop and Miss Ann Bishop, Maurice's mother and sister.

42. Minutes of CC meeting, June 6, 1981 (GD unnumbered), p. 3; minutes of CC meeting, July 8, 1981 (GD unnumbered), p. 1; minutes of CC meeting, December 30, 1981 (GD 104060), p. 3; "Summary of the Workings of the Central Committee from December 30th, 1981–February 12th, 1982" (GD 103745), p. 2; minutes of CC meeting, April 21, 1982 (GD 104060), p. 8; Bishop notes of CC meetings on July 19 and September 14, 1983.

43. "Minutes of Extra-Ordinary Meeting of the Central Committee of NJM from Tuesday 12th–Friday 15th October, 1982" (GD 000184); Bishop notes of same meeting. The account of this meeting is derived entirely from these two sources.

44. "Central Committee Report on First Plenary Session 13–19 July,

1983" (GD 100243); "Minutes of the Central Committee Plenary, 13–18 July, 1983" (GD unnumbered); Bishop notes of same meeting.

45. "Minutes of Emergency Meeting of NJM Central Committee Dated 26th August, 1983" (GD 100319).

46. Bishop notes of CC plenary meeting, September 14–15, 1983; Bernard Diederich, "Interviewing George Louison: A PRG Minister Talks About the Killings," *Caribbean Review*, vol.12, no. 4 (Fall 1983), pp. 17–18.

47. Minutes of CC plenary meeting, September 19–23, 1983 (GD 100277); "Extraordinary General Meeting of Full Members, Date: Sunday 25th September, 1983" (GD unnumbered).

48. "Extraordinary General Meeting . . . 25th September, 1983"; "The Central Committee of the NJM Held an Extraordinary C.C. Meeting on Friday August 26th, 1983, Just One Month After the Date of the July Plenary" (GD 000188).

49. "Extraordinary General Meeting . . . 25th September, 1983."

50. *Ibid.*

51. *Ibid.*

52. Notes on CC meeting, October 12, 1983, in Maurice Bishop's hand (GD 103764); "Report on the Meeting of PB & CC Held on Oct. 12th Given by Cde. Strachan," handwritten notes, author unknown (GD 000149); Steve Clark, "Introduction: Grenada's Workers' and Farmers' Government: Its Achievements and Its Overthrow," in Marcus and Louison.

53. "Year of Political and Academic Education," leaflet distributed to PRA troops, dated October 6, 1983 (GD 101020).

54. Clark, "Grenada's Workers' and Farmers' Government," p. xxxiv; "Vince Predicts Bloodshed," letter of Vincent Noel dated October 17, 1983, recounting his experiences of the last several days including meetings with Bishop, reprinted in *Grenadian Voice*, January 28, February 4, February 11, and February 18, 1984, p. 9 (all issues); handwritten letter to "Cde. Leader" from Nazim Burke, dated October 11, 1983 (GD 105144).

55. Clark, "Grenada's Workers' and Farmers' Government," pp. xxxiv–xxxv; Bishop notes on CC meeting, October 12, 1983; "Resolution of the People's Revolutionary Armed Forces Branch of the New JEWEL Movement (GD 000124); conversation with George Louison.

56. "Interrogation with St. Paul," conducted by Liam James, undated (GD 100263); signed confession of Errol George, dated October 12, 1983 (GD 000329); conversation with Alimenta Bishop.

57. Bishop notes of CC meeting, October 12, 1983.

GRENADA: THE UNTOLD STORY

58. *Ibid.*
59. *Ibid.*
60. *Ibid.;* diaries of unidentified persons, apparently an army officer (GD 000329) and two CC members (GD 101700, 104778); "Vince Predicts Bloodshed"; conversation with Alimenta Bishop.
61. "Report on the Meeting of PB & CC Held on Oct. 12th" (this manuscript goes on to provide minutes of the October 13 general meeting).
62. Diary of putative CC member (GD 101700); news release announcing Coard's resignation (GD 000181); Clark, "Grenada Workers' and Farmers' Government," p. xxxv.
63. Reports submitted to Major Keith Roberts during the period October 15–18, 1983 (GD 103691); diary of putative CC member (GD 104778), entry regarding briefing of Ambassador Rizo; letter from Fidel Castro to the NJM Central Committee, dated October 15, 1983 (GD unnumbered); Clark, "Grenada's Workers' and Farmers' Government," p. xxxvi.
64. Clark, "Grenada's Workers' and Farmers' Government," pp. xxxvi–xxxvii; Diederich, "Interviewing George Louison"; reports to Keith Roberts; handwritten resignations of Whiteman, Louison, Ramdhanny, and Norris Bain (GD 003212); conversation with Lyden Ramdhanny.
65. Diary of putative CC member (GD 104778); conversations with George Louison and others.
66. Clark, "Grenada's Workers' and Farmers' Government," p. xxxvii; conversations with George Louison, Lyden Ramdhanny, Brother Leonard, and many others.
67. Clark, "Grenada's Workers' and Farmers' Government," pp. xxxvii–xxxviii; O'Shaughnessy, *Grenada*, pp. 135–138; conversations with numerous Grenadians. The following account is based on the same sources.

SIX
Conclusion

If there ever was a real Grenadian revolution, it occurred on
October 19, 1983, when the people of Grenada seized upon
Maurice Bishop as the symbol of their sovereignty and tried to
impose him on the Central Committee. That this one-day revolution was so quickly and brutally suppressed shows that Grenada,
under the NJM, had long since become a country in which power
lay not with the "masses" or the "workers" or even the majority
of voters, but with the people who controlled the guns.

The history of the "Ruling Military Council," established as a
front for Coard's rump Central Committee in the wake of Bishop's
murder, was short and dismal. As the island convulsed with
horror at the assassinations, the party elite at Fort Frederick
immediately took steps to contain the expected popular reaction.
The fire department was called in to hose down the smoldering
vehicles and wash away the blood in the courtyard of Fort
Rupert, and a truck was commandeered to haul away the stacks
of bodies under the cover of darkness. To this day, no accurate
accounting has been made of the number of people who died.
Maurice Bishop's body has never been found. Hudson Austin
called in a Dr. Jensen Otway and dictated to him the cause of

death he was to record on forged post-mortem reports for nine bodies that had already been buried. PRA soldiers began rounding up known Bishop supporters and prospective dissidents, including leaders of the crowd at the October 19 demonstrations, people who had spoken out too openly at Worker Education sessions, and journalist Alistair Hughes. They were all packed into a small cell at Richmond Hill prison.[1]

The Ruling Military Council (RMC) was publicly announced by Hudson Austin over Radio Grenada at 9:00 p.m. the evening of the 19th. At the same time, he announced a 24-hour-a-day curfew, violators of which were to be shot on sight. The RMC consisted mostly of the officer corps, including CC members James, Layne, and Cornwall. Unbeknownst to the outside world the Central Committee itself continued to meet daily in Fort Frederick to map out a strategy for the difficult days ahead.

As a first priority, the army issued bulletins to the troops explaining what had happened at Fort Rupert and commending the soldiers on their heroism. The official line was that Maurice Bishop "and other people of the bourgeois and upper bourgeois strata" had forced their way into PRA headquarters and had begun distributing arms to the masses. They allegedly beat up and stripped several PRA women in the Fort and were making plans to murder all the party members, officers, and NCOs they held. They had, according to propaganda line, intended to build a new party and army "to defend the interest of the bourgeois." Four soldiers who had died in the assault on the Fort (probably from the misdirected fire of their comrades) were honored as heroes of the revolution.[2]

Key steps for restoring the internal situation were to be an official period of mourning, a promise of a civilian government within two weeks (the CC had already chosen names by October 20), a temporary lifting of the curfew to allow people to buy food, and the resumption of normal government business on Monday, October 24. Any government employees failing to show up for work on that date would be subject to "firm disciplinary action," although the curfew would continue in effect from 6 p.m. to 6 a.m. Ministry personnel would be given specific tasks to do to occupy their time and prevent them from dwelling on their shock over recent events. Above all, one CC member wrote, "patriotism" was the key to a return to normalcy.[3]

Patriotism was a particularly important theme in view of the Central Committee's fear of an invasion. While trying to present to the outside world a picture of continued civil order, and promising imminent appointment of a broad-based civilian government, the RMC worked frantically to whip up overseas support for its regime. The Council sent messages to friendly countries and "fraternal parties" around the Caribbean and the world, conveying the official line on Bishop's treachery. Feelers went out to non-socialist Caribbean countries like Trinidad and St. Vincent, all but pleading for private meetings to explain the RMC's position. These efforts were in vain. Grenada's neighbors were outraged. Tom Adams of Barbados called the murders at Fort Rupert "the most vicious act to disfigure the West Indies since the days of slavery." Dominica's Eugenia Charles refused to have dealings with Grenada's "unlawfully" constituted regime. In Jamaica, Prime Minister Seaga referred to his government's "revulsion" at a system which had produced "murderers in high places of leadership," while the former socialist Prime Minister, Michael Manley, called the murders "a squalid betrayal of the hopes of the ordinary people of our region."[4]

Only the Soviet Union was completely supportive, a fact for which the leaders in St. George's were deeply grateful. (The Soviets' support has raised speculation that Coard consulted with them before moving against Bishop). Castro was livid. On October 25 he broadcast a formal statement distancing himself from the regime in St. George's, declaring that "No doctrine, no principle or position held up as revolutionary, and no internal division justifies atrocious proceedings like the physical elimination of Bishop and the . . . worthy leaders killed yesterday." The guilty parties, he said, should be "punished in an exemplary way." The CC leaders were stunned by this savage rebuke from Grenada's most vital ally. They quickly circulated among the party faithful the official interpretation that Fidel's friendship for Bishop had blinded him to the dishonesty and wickedness of the Bishop group, and led him to take a personal rather than a *class* approach to the events.[5]

Indications on the home front were also unsettling. The curfew prevented any resistance from organizing for the time being. But efforts to disarm the militia had been only partially effective and the potential for armed insurrection was very real. One leader recorded in his notebook at an October 22 Central Committee meeting that "control of civil disorder, sabotage, and terrorism" was a top priority. Another noted that the "internal situation is perfect" for outside intervention. Even the PRA was not completely reliable, as indicated by an October 23 diary entry reading "army coup imminent against General [Austin]." The media in Barbados also picked up rumors to this effect. According to one recent publication in which survivors of the Bishop group collaborated, Kenrick Radix, George Louison, and Don Rojas were all convinced that in the absence of the US/OECS intervention, civil war would soon have broken out, aimed at toppling the Coard regime.[6]

This is highly plausible. Less plausible is the pro-Bishop group's contention that it stood a good chance of winning a civil war quickly. In the absence of any central coordination or a recognized leader of Bishop's stature, the more probable result would have been protracted bloodletting and deepening social chaos that would have ended only when the Cubans had intervened to impose a solution. That the Cubans would have been willing to intervene is suggested by a number of facts. Among the most persuasive is that the Cubans in Grenada were already at the point of intervening on Bishop's behalf on October 19. According to Lyden Ramdhanny, Ambassador Rizo contacted Bishop twice offering help, once in person during his house arrest and once by a message carried to Fort Rupert in the last hour of the Prime Minister's life. Both times Bishop restrained Rizo's hand, preferring as ever to deal with internal party matters internally. A personal letter from a Cuban soldier to his family, tells that "on the 19th I was selected to go on a rescue mission of Bishop but when we were prepared the news arrived that they had shot him along with his companions."[7]

There can be little doubt that under any NJM regime that emerged after October 1983, whether dominated by Coard or by a Cuban-backed Bishop faction, Grenada would have moved further toward communism, relying on ever more forthright repression to hold down an increasingly disaffected populace. Its deepening military and economic dependence on the socialist bloc would have completed Grenada's isolation from its democratic neighbors and accelerated its development as a center for training and support of insurgent movements throughout the region. The US/OECS intervention cut short this development. When American and Caribbean forces landed in Grenada in what the vast majority of Grenadians welcomed as a "rescue operation," they encountered an army that already dwarfed those of all Grenada's OECS neighbors put together, and was scheduled for significant further expansion.[8]

While the existence of such a disproportionate military force undoubtedly posed a threat to other small islands, there is little evidence that the PRG planned any direct aggression against its neighbors. At some future time, especially after the completion of the international airport, Grenada might have served as a forward supply base for Cuban-sponsored insurrection in parts of Latin America; and the PRG would doubtless have been tempted to lend military aid to any really promising revolutionary movement in a nearby island. The main purpose of this arsenal though, seems to have been to provide security for the revolution itself; or more accurately, to provide symbols of security and tokens of power to men who, having destroyed the foundations for the rule of law in their society, had become ever more preoccupied with sheer force as the basis for their regime.[9]

When the long-feared military intervention came, it was not a response to the PRG's constant rhetorical provocations, nor to its pro-Soviet activities, nor even to the local threat of its ongoing military buildup. It came as a result of the regime's own internal disintegration into chaos and bloodshed, as the paranoia and ruthlessness in which the NJM leaders had indoctrinated themselves so assiduously, turned inward. Far from being a violation of Grenada's sovereignty, it was a restoration of sovereignty to the Grenadian people vis-à-vis a regime which had lost any trace of a legitimate mandate it might once have enjoyed.

Teddy Victor, co-founder of the original JEWEL, once remarked that "the NJM was born in deception and died in deception." The party won popular support in its early days because of its program of social justice; it lost support as Grenadians began to realize that it was not, and would never become, what it had claimed to be. The party offered neither national liberation, nor a solution to economic problems and unemployment, nor a path to a more humane society. Knowing that the Grenadian people would never willingly accept their real program or ideology, the NJM's communist leaders deliberately concealed the character of their movement from the public, and even (especially in the early days) from rank-and-file party members.

Yet there was an ambiguity in the NJM that persisted to the end, and became almost a schizophrenia in leaders like Bishop, Whiteman and some of their colleagues. They wanted their revolution to be genuinely popular, and continued to expect that Marxism-Leninism would serve as a means to improve the lot of the Grenadian people. Some had occasional moments of doubt about the long-range dangers of excessive secrecy, as did a Grenadian envoy in Cuba (probably Richard Jacobs) who wrote to Bishop in 1980 in reference to the troubles with the "Budhlall Gang":

> We must tell the people the *whole truth*.... Such an approach I know means sacrificing certain not so well kept secrets about the ideological orientation of the leadership before, and after, our revolution.... But the preoccupation with secrecy of our ultimate political goal ... could well be considered to have outlived its usefulness....[10]

It was this sort of soft-headedness that frustrated and offended Coard and his fellow adherents of Leninist "principle." They realized that a Marxist-Leninist system on the Soviet model could not be constructed except through the most rigidly centralized control by an ideologically committed elite. *They* were never deceived that theirs could be a truly popular revolution. Coard, moreover, was a true ascetic revolutionary. His commitment was not to improving the well-being of Grenada, or of any specific country, but rather to building an international communist society, whatever short-term human sacrifice might be involved. He had fully accepted, as Bishop apparently had not, that Grenada's "backwardness" meant that the masses would have to be led to communism by a combination of force and fraud. When deception failed—when propaganda became too inconsistent with reality to be believed—only ruthless coercion could hold the revolution on course.

The NJM's failure to resolve this conflict between populism and communism contributed to its self-destruction. The persistence of Bishop as a popular leader long after the party had moved beyond him ideologically was an aggravating factor. But the NJM's fundamental failures, its bungled social programs, its ruinous economic policy, its accelerating repression, its politicization of every area of life, and its near-complete loss of the popular support it once had were not failures of specific individuals. The failures were the result of an ill-conceived attempt to transform Grenada into a slavish imitation of a Cuban-style state.

NOTES

1. O'Shaughnessy, *Grenada*, pp. 141–144; conversations with Grenadians.
2. "Revolutionary Soldiers and Men of the People's Revolutionary Armed Forces," leaflet dated October 19, 1983 (GD 000096); "Bulletin from the Main Political Department: Their Heroism is an Example for Us," leaflet dated October 20, 1983 (GD 000100); diaries of putative CC members (GD 104778, 101700); O'Shaughnessy, *Grenada*, p. 140.
3. Diary of putative CC member (GD 104778); minutes of CC meeting, October 20, 1983 (GD unnumbered).
4. Diary of putative CC member (GD 101700); handwritten draft (author unknown) of message to Government of St. Vincent to try to arrange meeting on Carriacou with General Austin (GD 105598); handwritten draft (author unknown) of message to the Soviet Union (GD 105598); Greaves, "The Grenada Document," pp. 25–26.
5. "Statement by the Cuban Government and the Cuban Communist Party," in Marcus and Taber, *Maurice Bishop Speaks*, pp. 313–316; "On Cuba's Response to the Issue," handwritten draft of official CC position on Castro's statement (GD 000015). The Workers' Party of Jamaica (WPJ), whose members in Grenada had been in

constant touch with Trevor Munroe during the leadership crisis and had apparently tried to mediate it, also drafted a statement supportive of Coard and his followers.

6. Diaries of putative CC members (GD 104778, 101700, 000329); Clark, "Grenada's Workers' and Farmers' Government," p. xxxix.

7. Clark, "Grenada's Workers' and Farmers' Government," p. xxxix; letter from Cuban construction worker to his family in Havana province (GD 000426); conversation with Lyden Ramdhanny.

8. U.S., *Grenada: A Preliminary Report*, pp. 18–21.

9. Caribbean scholar Selwyn Ryan, in a paper prepared for a May 1984 conference on Grenada at the University of the West Indies in Trinidad, made the following pertinent observation: "It was indeed ironic, though understandable, that a regime which came to power through the use of violence should see no ideological contradiction in seeking to eliminate others who were suspected of seeking to do the same thing. And that is one of the main flaws in the argument which dismisses elections as mere routine. Despite all the justified criticisms which are levelled against Westminster type elections, they are nonetheless part of a package of norms and practices which are mutually reinforcing, and once they are dismissed as irrelevant, there is nothing else which cannot be withdrawn in the name of the people's democracy, guided democracy or some other variant" ("Grenada: Balance Sheet of the Revolution," p. 4).

10. Letter from Embassy of Grenada in Havana to "Comrade Leader," unsigned, dated August 14, 1980 (GD 000914).